A CONVERSATION BOOK 2B
English in Everyday Life
Third Edition

Tina Kasloff Carver
Sandra Douglas Fotinos

Prentice Hall Regents
A VIACOM COMPANY

Prentice Hall Regents
Upper Saddle River, New Jersey 07458

Publisher: *Louisa B. Hellegers*
Development Editors: *Gino Mastascusa, Barbara Barysh, Janet Johnston*
Director of Production and Manufacturing: *Aliza Greenblatt*
Executive Managing Editor: *Dominick Mosco*

Electronic Production Editors: *Janice Sivertsen, Ken Liao, Christine Mann*
Production Assistant: *Christine Lauricella*
Electronic Art Production Supervisor: *Ken Liao*
Electronic Publishing Specialist: *Steven Greydanus*
Art Director: *Merle Krumper*
Manufacturing Manager: *Ray Keating*

Illustrator: *Andrew Lange*

© 1998 by Prentice Hall Regents
Prentice-Hall, Inc.
A Simon & Schuster Company
Upper Saddle River, New Jersey 07458

All rights reserved. No part of this book may be reproduced, in any form or by any means, without permission in writing from the publisher.

Printed in the United States of America
10 9 8 7 6 5 4 3 2 1

0-13-792532-8

Prentice-Hall International (UK) Limited, *London*
Prentice-Hall of Australia Pty. Limited, *Sydney*
Prentice-Hall Canada Inc., *Toronto*
Prentice-Hall Hispanoamericana, S.A., *Mexico*
Prentice-Hall of India Private Limited, *New Delhi*
Prentice-Hall of Japan, Inc., *Tokyo*
Simon & Schuster Asia Pte. Ltd., *Singapore*
Editora Prentice-Hall do Brasil, Ltda., *Rio de Janeiro*

CONTENTS

FOREWORD ix
ACKNOWLEDGMENTS x
TO THE TEACHER xiii
TO THE STUDENT xix
WELCOME TO CLASS! xxii

UNIT 1: HOUSING 1

LESSON	COMPETENCY OBJECTIVES	PAGE
Places to Live	• compare and contrast advantages and disadvantages of living in different locations, kinds of housing, and renting or buying a house	2
Inside Your Home	• discuss special individual housing needs; explain decorating preferences	4
Finding the Right Home	• read and discuss ads for housing; discuss what to look for when renting an apartment or buying a house	6
Utility Problems	• discuss mistakes people make with utilities and how to avoid these problems; discuss different kinds of heating and air conditioning across cultures	8
Tenants and Landlords	• compare and contrast rights and responsibilities of tenants and landlords; discuss problems between tenants and landlords and recommend solutions	10
Insuring Your Property	• identify and discuss common problems resulting in property damage or loss; discuss insurance coverage across cultures	12
Moving	• identify and discuss reasons for moving and the process and problems of moving; ask and tell about experiences with moving	14
Answering the Door	• identify and discuss reasons why people come to your door and what to say when they do	16
Neighborhood Problems	• identify and discuss neighborhood problems and solutions in general and in your neighborhood in particular; find out what your community is doing to solve the problems	10
Neighborhood Improvements	• identify and discuss neighborhood improvements; discuss ways to be neighborly; compare and contrast neighborhoods and neighbors across cultures	20
Review		22

iii

UNIT 2: TRANSPORTATION AND TRAVEL 23

LESSON	COMPETENCY OBJECTIVES	PAGE
Commuting	• identify different forms of commuting; discuss advantages and disadvantages of each	24
Learning to Drive	• discuss procedures and problems of learning to drive and taking driving tests	26
Driving Problems	• identify and discuss common problems of driving, what to do about them, and how to avoid them; discuss an automobile insurance policy	28
Buying a Car	• discuss preferences and priorities in selecting a car, and what to do and say when buying a car	30
On Vacation	• compare preferences for vacation travel; state own travel wishes or plans	32
Traveling by Car	• identify and discuss procedures and highlights of long-distance car travel; compare and contrast car travel across cultures	34
Bus and Train Travel	• discuss advantages and disadvantages of bus and train transportation; ask and answer questions about personal experiences with buses and trains	36
Air Travel	• identify and discuss procedures and common problems associated with air travel	38
Review		40

UNIT 3: FINDING A JOB 41

LESSON	COMPETENCY OBJECTIVES	PAGE
Jobs in Your Community	• identify and discuss occupations; inquire about jobs and types of businesses and industries in the community; identify and discuss employment opportunities	42
Your Occupation	• ask and answer questions about classmates' jobs; explain present job duties	46
The Right Job for you	• ask and answer questions about job preferences	48
Looking for a Job	• discuss different ways to finding a job; find out about job openings through want ads; discuss advantages and disadvantages of jobs; discuss abilities, experience, and job needs of classmates	50
Applying for a Job	• discuss job interview scenarios; prepare questions that an interviewer and applicant would ask; respond to employment interview questions, including short- and long-term employment goals, qualifications, and previous job duties	52
Wages and Benefits	• identify and discuss wages and benefits; express preferences regarding wages and benefits; discuss reasons to ask for a raise	54
Review		56

UNIT 4: LIFE AT WORK — 57

LESSON	COMPETENCY OBJECTIVES	PAGE
Starting a New Job	• identify and discuss common problems in a new job and possible solutions; tell about a job experience	58
Instructions at Work	• give and follow multi-step instructions to complete a task; identify and discuss common problems giving and following instructions	60
Doing a Good Job	• identify and discuss common problems at work and acceptable and unacceptable work behavior; provide solutions to problems and give advice to workers	62
Injuries at Work	• discuss common work-related injuries, hazards at work and at home, workmen's compensation, and procedures for preventing and dealing with injuries on the job	64
Deductions from Pay	• identify and discuss paycheck deductions; understand basic payroll deductions	66
Spending Money	• discuss advantages and disadvantages of different spending patterns; clarify and/or reconfirm own personal spending patterns	68
Paying Taxes	• discuss concepts and procedures for paying income tax; understand basic terminology of income tax; compare and contrast taxes in different countries	70
Leaving a Job	• identify and discuss common reasons for leaving a job; clarify and consider options	72
Review		74

UNIT 5: IN THE NEWS   75

LESSON	COMPETENCY OBJECTIVES	PAGE
Class News	• ask and tell about personal life events	76
News Media	• identify and discuss varieties of news media; discuss people and stories in the news	78
Weather and Natural Disasters	• identify different kinds of severe weather and natural disasters; ask and answer questions about personal experiences involving a natural disaster	80
Sports News	• identify and discuss issues related to sports in the news; discuss popularity of sports and athletes in different countries	82
Entertainment News	• identify and discuss various kinds of entertainment available locally; make arrangements with class to attend an event together	84
Crime in the News	• identify and discuss crimes and criminal justice; share cross-cultural opinions about criminal justice	86
Heroes in the News	• identify and discuss heroes across time and cultures; explain personal ideals of heroism	88
Local News	• identify and discuss local events in the news; become familiar with local issues	90
World News	• identify and discuss events in the news around the world; become familiar with international issues	92
Politics and Government in the News	• identify and discuss characteristics of politics and government	94
Review		96

APPENDIX   97
Conversation Springboards   98
Grammar for Conversation Contents   114
Grammar for Conversation   115
Maps   125
Speech/Audience Evaluation Forms   130
Activities Guide   131
Alphabetical Word List to Picture Dictionary   142

FOREWORD

Almost immediately after the Third Edition of **A CONVERSATION BOOK 1**—featuring a picture dictionary format with a variety of student-centered material—was published in 1994, we started receiving requests for a split edition which would spread the material in **Books 1** and **2** over a four-semester sequence with the addition of sample conversations and a grammar-for-conversation reference section. **A CONVERSATION BOOK 1** is now available in both full and split editions (1A and 1B). This new edition of **A CONVERSATION BOOK 2** is the second half of our response to the many teachers who wrote or talked to us. It is designed to cover the third and fourth semesters of the four-semester sequence and to complete the series started with **A CONVERSATION BOOK 1**, providing flexibility while sacrificing none of the content or spirit of the original.

This Third Edition of **A CONVERSATION BOOK 2** is therefore available in both full and split editions. Both editions have Conversation Springboards and Grammar for Conversation sections in the Appendix, and the Conversation Springboards as well as the discrete vocabulary are also available on audiotape cassettes. A page-for-page spiral-bound Teacher's Guide with teaching suggestions and additional activities for each lesson, plus tests for each unit, is available for each book.

The new edition remains true to the original concept of **A CONVERSATION BOOK**: that students acquire conversation skills best when their own experiences and interests are part of the conversation, and that student-centered, cross-cultural materials with extensive vocabulary and engaging illustrations focused on everyday life and the community they live in can help make the learning process a pleasure. We hope that **A CONVERSATION BOOK 2, THIRD EDITION** will help to make your conversation class a meaningful, enjoyable, and memorable learning experience for you and your students.

ACKNOWLEDGMENTS

No book is written in isolation. We could never begin to cite all the teachers we have spoken with, the programs we have observed, and the authors who have influenced the writing of this book. They all have been part of our education and developing expertise as authors. We are indebted to them all, as well as to those teachers and students who have used the last two editions of the **CONVERSATION BOOK**.

The process of getting a book from first concept to press and out to the classroom involves many people. We were fortunate to have dedicated, competent support during this time. For the Third Edition, which is the basis of the Revised Edition, our sincere appreciation goes to Nancy Baxer, our editor, who encouraged us to recreate the **CONVERSATION BOOKS** in a new way and whose vision and tenacity supported the process. Andrew Lange, our artist and the designer of the book, has continually surprised and delighted us with the creativity and humor of his work. For examples of Andrew's imagination unleashed, look at the title page of each unit. We asked Andrew to draw whatever he wanted for those pages, and every unit surpassed the ones that came before! The result is a new artistic pedagogy—a major focus of change in the Third Edition.

For the long process of shaping our pages into a complex and complete finished product, our sincere thanks and great appreciation must go first to Gino Mastascusa, our development editor, who became our partner in every way. Gino's dedication, creativity, attention to detail, diplomacy, and long hours and unflagging hard work can be seen in every page. No words of thanks are really adequate. Kudos to you, Gino. Barbara Barysh, who helped in so many ways in the Third Edition, lent a superb editorial eye to this revision by catching so many inconsistencies and suggesting ways to make the materials more easily taught. And to Janet Johnston we owe a great debt of thanks for her expertise on the Grammar for Conversation sections.

In a text such as this, production qualities are of utmost importance. The appeal to the student, the "look" as well as the accessibility, contribute to its pedagogy almost as much as the content itself. We'd like to thank the production team that worked so professionally on the book: Ken Liao and Jan Sivertsen for the beautiful interior pages, Christine Mann for her wonderful design of the Grammar for Conversation pages as well as the rest of the front and back matter, Carey Davies for his additional technical support and extraordinary revisions of the maps, Steven Greydanus for his finely tuned "tweaks" to the art, and Christine Lauricella for her excellent preparation of the tapescripts.

Our appreciation goes to Ki Chul Kang, who for years gathered information and suggestions from teachers in Asia and who helped mold this new revision. Also, Steven Golden, Stephen Troth, Gunawan Hadi, Jerene Tan—thanks for your support both now and over the years, and for your thoughtful recommendations on the Conversation Springboards. Without you, this edition would never have been created!

Our sincere thanks to Louisa Hellegers, our publisher, who responded to the requests from the field and helped mold them into reality. Because of Louisa's belief in this project, these texts have been published with the values and the timeliness they need.

Our thanks to Professor H. Douglas Brown, who guided us through the Learning Strategies for every unit and wrote the To the Student.

The list could go on and on—and fearful that we have omitted someone, we thank also Tom Dare, Mike Bennett, Gordon Johnson, Susan Fesler, Rob Walters, and Maria Angione. Also, thanks to Andy Martin and Gil Muller, as well as to H.T. Jennings, Karen Chiang, and Norman Harris, for their professional contributions and personal support.

Our own personal experiences as ESL teachers and foreign language learners underlie every page of **A CONVERSATION BOOK 2**. As learners living and working in other countries, we were reminded daily that learning a new culture and a new language is very hard work! To the many people who afforded us friendship when we were far from home, helped us deal with the complexity of everyday life in a new place, and patiently shared perceptions and languages with us, thank you. Without those experiences and without those people to guide us, **CONVERSATION BOOKS** 1 and 2 would never have been written.

A Personal Word from Tina Carver

It is rare that an *editor* is afforded the opportunity to thank *authors*, but this time the role reversal is appropriate. I have the good fortune to have been the colleague and editor for authors who professionally exhibit the highest level of excellence to which I aspire, and who, through the years, have also become very good friends. I will always value that friendship. So, to Betty Azar, Bill Bliss, Doug Brown, and Steve Molinsky, thank you—much of the improvement in this revision is the result of the many years of our professional conversations and work together.

A special note of appreciation goes to Sandra Fotinos, my master teacher of so many years ago, whose expert teaching and instincts toward students' needs have set an example to me throughout my career. Through all these years and experiences, both personal and professional, we have remained friends and colleagues.

I would like to express my appreciation to my three children, Jeffrey, Brian, and Daniel, who grew up with the **CONVERSATION BOOKS** as youngsters. Now that they are young adults, their daily help and understanding—from reading the manuscript and offering suggestions to doing the cooking, laundry, shopping, and walking the dogs—made my work easier and, indeed, possible. My mother and father, Ruth and George Kasloff, influenced my early decision-making. My mother has continued to guide and to support me in all my endeavors. Finally, I would like to express my appreciation to Gene Podhurst for his support through the long process of this revision.

A Personal Word from Sandra Fotinos-Riggs

I would like to thank my colleagues at Cochise College, Northern Essex Community College, and Harvard University for the many good years of stories and teaching techniques that we have shared, and for the constant, gentle reminder that what works once does not necessarily work again in another class or for another teacher.

For whatever I have really learned of living across cultures and languages through the delights and the hard times of everyday life, I want to say thank you to my Fotinos family-by-marriage and especially to my mother-in-law, Kleopatra Fotinou, of Kallitsaina, Messinias, who for more than thirty years was my Greek teacher and a loving, understanding friend.

Finally, thank you again to my children, Christina, Elizabeth, and Paul, who, like Tina's children, grew up with the **CONVERSATION BOOKS** and whose cross-cultural life experiences are imbedded in so many of the conversations of the books. And for the personal support without which this revision would have been impossible, thank you to Gene Riggs, my incredibly patient husband, and to Tina Carver, for twenty-five years my co-author and friend.

New York/Arizona
October 1997

TO THE TEACHER

These notes are provided as springboards for your own creativity and initiative. We have revised **A CONVERSATION BOOK 2** to incorporate new English teaching methods with those that have worked successfully through the years. Our intention is to provide a wide variety of vocabulary and student-centered learning activities for you to use within your own style and that of your intermediate ESL/EFL students.

Equally important to these activities is creating an atmosphere of shared learning in which students' differences are valued and their life experiences are appreciated. We have endeavored to create materials that will foster the idea that the class is a partnership between teacher and student and between student and student.

LEARNING STRATEGIES

The Learning Strategies box on the first page of every unit suggests three or four ways to facilitate learning for the unit. These are meant as springboards to get students thinking about the best ways for them to learn. This small section is designed to guide students to understand, appreciate, develop, and broaden their own learning styles. The learning strategies encourage critical thinking and discovery of personal learning styles, both of which are essential to becoming a self-aware and independent learner.

Read the introduction from Professor H. Douglas Brown with the class and discuss the advantages of understanding how each individual has his or her own way to learn most effectively. Then, as you begin each unit, discuss the learning strategies for that unit. Have students concentrate on the strategies throughout the unit, and have them continue to practice the strategies from previous units. Add strategies as everyone in the class becomes aware of his or her unique learning style.

Integrate the teaching of independent learning skills throughout the course. To help students organize their learning tasks, have each student bring a notebook to class and divide it into four tabbed sections: Vocabulary, Dialog Journal, Community Information, and Activities. When new words are generated in the classroom from discussion or from activities, students should record the words and information about them in the Vocabulary section of their notebooks. Write new words and sentences on the board so that students can record them accurately. The Dialog Journal section should be set aside for journal entries, both those suggested in the text and other topics you—or the students—may choose. The Community Information section should be a place to note valuable information about the students' communities and could be used as a handy reference tool outside the classroom. The Activities section should be used for any activities the students do in class or at home. There are specific suggestions in the Teacher's Edition and the student text as to how and when to use the notebook.

ILLUSTRATIONS AND ACTIVITIES

Our "mascot" appears again in **A CONVERSATION BOOK 2**. Use him as a whimsical thread throughout the course. Giving the mascot a name has proven a valuable activity at the beginning of **A CONVERSATION BOOK 1**; it should be continued in Book 2.

The illustrations serve as a visual entrance into each lesson, presenting the vocabulary and concept of the lesson in the context of real-life situations. Some of these situations are presented as problems, others as stories—with and without endings. All are designed to stimulate discussion through the first activity of each lesson: Picture Discussion.

Subsequent activities tie the lessons' illustrations to the students' lives and interests in a variety of ways, such as through role plays, story telling, problem solving, brainstorming, and memory games.

There are many kinds of activities in this book. Step-by-step instructions for leading students through each kind of activity are included on pages 131 through 141 in the Appendix.

CONVERSATION SPRINGBOARDS

Here are dialogs for teachers who hate dialogs! We have developed these springboards as conversation starters, to serve as models and inspirations for students to talk about their life experiences. These conversations are NOT listen/repeat dialogs! They are NOT designed to be used for pattern practice. They are intentionally longer and more difficult than traditional dialogs because they are meant for listening to and understanding real, whole conversations about everyday life in English. They are designed as samples of native-speaker conversations, above the level of conversation that the students could be expected to produce themselves. In fact, they replicate the situation that ESL and EFL students most often find themselves in with native speakers of English, where the conversation is fast and full of idioms, and the students have to cope with understanding and participating at their own level.

An accompanying Audio Program is available that includes all of these Conversation Springboards. Cassette icons on student-text pages signal where to use the audiotape. Each icon is footnoted with a cross-reference to the Appendix page with the corresponding Conversation Springboards; each type has a specific purpose.

- *What's the process?* Conversation Springboards are to be used before specified activities, and are intended to help students understand and talk about the purpose and process of the activity, as well as possible complications and their solutions.
- *What's happening?* Conversation Springboards tell a story happening in the present. These dialogs are intended to help students listen to conversational narratives in present time, and to retell stories chronologically, using present and present progressive tenses.
- *What happened?* Conversation Springboards relate a story that happened in the past and give students practice listening to past-time narratives and retelling the events in order, using past tenses.
- *What's next?* Conversation Springboards tell a story without an ending, or with a next step implied but not stated. They give students practice in drawing conclusions from indirect information, as well as opportunities to create their own endings in future time.
- *What's your opinion?* Conversation Springboards present a situation where preferences and opinions are expressed, and give students opportunities to agree or disagree with others' opinions, express their own opinions, and participate in a class discussion of a topic.
- *Picture Springboards* are incomplete conversations between two or more characters in one of the pictures in the lesson. At the end of each conversation are blank lines for students to complete the conversation. There is one Picture Springboard for each lesson in this book.

We suggest the following method of using the Conversation Springboards and accompanying Audio Program:

1. Listen to the entire conversation once with books open or closed, depending on the class level and your preference. (Students with very limited vocabulary may find it reassuring to preread the conversation at home before class.)

2. Listen again, breaking up the conversation by stopping the tape after every two lines. Check for understanding. Define any words or phrases that are unclear. Whenever possible, have students write down unclear words and try to guess the meaning from context.

3. Listen to the entire dialog again. (If you have listened with books closed until now, listen this time with books open.)

4. Follow up by having students either explain the process, situation, or problem, tell the story, or finish the conversation, depending on which type of Conversation Springboard you are using.

5. You may wish to have students read the conversations out loud. If you do, go slowly!

VOCABULARY

Every lesson has a vocabulary box listing some of the basic vocabulary for the lesson, plus spaces for students to add words. Following the picture dictionary format of **A CONVERSATION BOOK 1**, each word in the vocabulary box is related to the art of the lesson, and is also included for practice on the audiotape for that lesson. Words already presented in **A CONVERSATION BOOK 1** Third Edition are not repeated in Book 2. Also, as in Book 1, each new word is listed only the first time it is used in the book. Keep this in mind if you are not using the book from beginning to end. Use the Index to find the words and their original page references. Take the opportunity to teach students how and when an index can be used in their studies.

To present the vocabulary, either have students look at the picture and call out the individual words they know, or begin by having students describe the scene. Then repeat the individual words and have students follow your cue.

Modeling the words for pronunciation is useful for students so they can hear how to say the word in English in conjunction with seeing the illustration and the written word. Although it may be difficult for you to hear all the pronunciations, choral repetition will give students an opportunity to verbalize the words they are learning. Be sure students understand all the words. Sometimes native language translation is appropriate; that is your judgment call!

Have students add to the vocabulary box with words they contribute to the class discussions. By adding the students' suggested words to the list, you are reinforcing their retention and recall of introductory-level vocabulary, encouraging them to explore new vocabulary, and validating their contributions to the class. The words may be ones that students already know or ones you provide as their "living dictionary." Or they may be words that students find in their bilingual dictionaries and then look up in their English/English dictionaries. At this level, students should begin to use an English-only dictionary to understand new vocabulary, rather than relying solely on their bilingual dictionaries. Help them ease into this important study skill by actively using English/English dictionaries in class.

A vocabulary problem common to intermediate-level English language students is predicting abstract noun and adjective forms and uses of a word from its basic verb form (permit/permission/permissive/permissible; resist/resistance/resistant; succeed/success/successful.) To begin to address this problem, we have included in some of the vocabulary lists varying word forms that are difficult to predict. Discuss and explore word families with your class as you expand the vocabulary lists together. It is always important to provide a meaningful context for each variant of a word (They want to succeed./Success in this course is important to them./They are successful students.) Have students experiment with uses of word variants themselves. Although the students will make mistakes, such guesses are essential to true vocabulary acquisition. This provides a good opportunity to encourage "risk-taking" tolerance.

The Word Families charts in the Grammar for Conversation section can be helpful in clarifying the idea of word families. Encourage students to keep their own "Word Families" lists in the Vocabulary section of their notebooks. In the Teacher's Edition, we have included additional activities for vocabulary expansion, retention, and recall.

GRAMMAR FOR CONVERSATION

In the Appendix, there are grammar paradigms for each unit, charted to illustrate useful patterns, phrases, and vocabulary from the unit. The grammar charts avoid complicated terminology and are meant to be quick references and springboards for incorporating grammar into conversation so that students can say what they really mean.

The conversations in this book are not grammar-based. On the contrary, the grammar emerges from the conversations. The practical needs of conversation in everyday life form the basis of the grammar included in this text. As a result, some of the grammar is out of sequence for a standard grammar-based approach, but is in sequence for real-life conversations. Any grammar that is "above" a student's grammar level can still be accessible as a usable set phrase, and all of the charts and lists are expandable for use in classes that are interested in talking about grammar.

CONVERSATION MONITOR

Some group activities call for a conversation monitor. The first time your class uses a conversation monitor, discuss what his/her functions will be and list those functions on the board (keeping the conversation going, covering the topics, being sure everyone gets a chance to contribute to the activity, organizing the "reporting back," etc.). Make sure that all students, not just the more outspoken students, take turns being conversation monitors. Practice with a demonstration group. Take the role of the monitor with the group. Narrate the role of the monitor as you are going through the activity.

RECORDER

While the conversation monitor's role is to keep the conversation going and to allow everyone to have a turn, the recorder is charged with taking notes on the various activities so there will be concrete written notes when it comes time to "report back to the class." It may help the class for you to play the recorder role at first and write the notes on the chalkboard as a model.

PRONUNCIATION

Encourage students to try to pronounce clearly but not to worry about trying to sound like native speakers of English. The students' emphasis should always be on communication and fluency in conversation. However, when pronunciation difficulty impedes communication, it is well worth focusing on a discrete point (e.g., can vs. can't). Role plays can also help improve pronunciation: often when students are pretending to be someone else, they are less inhibited about making "foreign" sounds. Pronunciation can be improved by repeating vocabulary words at the beginning of the lesson.

CORRECTIONS

Too much correction inhibits students' ability to think coherently and works contrary to developing integrated conversation skills. Teachers should aim to strike a balance, teaching syntax as well as pronunciation at opportune times. Make a note of the errors students are making. It is usually not helpful to interrupt the flow of students' conversations, but to correct errors at the appropriate time later in class, without referring to any specific student. Use your own judgment according to the individual student and the moment.

GROUPING

All activities require some type of grouping—pairs, triads, or groups of four, five, etc. As students get to know each other, informal methods of grouping usually work best. Occasionally, let students choose a partner or set up their own groups. For other activities, depending upon the subject, deliberately mix genders, age, language groups, occupations, or opinions. Try to avoid cliques sitting together. Remind students that the only way to develop conversational fluency in English is to practice in English!

CHALKBOARD

Because many students are visual learners, use the chalkboard as much as possible to encourage students to both see and hear the vocabulary, phrases, and sentences associated with the conversation topic. Write unfamiliar words on the board for students to copy in the Vocabulary section of their notebooks.

Use the board to expand the charts or grids in the text. Construct the chart or grid while students are engaged in the activity. Utilize the board so that all students' or all groups' information can be included. Also, use the board to write all the information generated from survey activities. Encourage students to come to the board and write also. Have students be "recorders" and write words on the board from time to time. This will build confidence and self-esteem.

WRITING

For follow-up activities that will give students a chance to write about many of the conversation topics, we suggest using the black line masters in **A WRITING BOOK**, a collection of one hundred complete writing lessons for using English in everyday life. Each lesson includes individual and/or cooperative writing tasks, such as writing letters, journals, notes, invitations, and shopping lists, and filling out forms. There is a cross-reference in the back of both **A WRITING BOOK** and **A CONVERSATION BOOK 2 TEACHER'S GUIDE** that correlates lessons in the two books.

TEACHER'S GUIDE

The page-for-page **TEACHER'S GUIDE** gives Warm-up and Expansion activities for each lesson, plus step-by-step suggestions for all the activities. It also includes a conversation test and a vocabulary test for each unit, as well as suggestions for administering the tests and for using them as teaching/learning tools. In addition, it provides a checklist of topics and skills covered in A **CONVERSATION BOOK 2** and correlations to writing activities in **A WRITING BOOK**.

TO THE STUDENT

In **A CONVERSATION BOOK 2**, your teacher will help you to learn English by using it in conversations with English speakers. Your work in the classroom is very important. It will help you to practice English, to speak more clearly and fluently, and to listen to others carefully and understand what they are saying. But it is also very important for you to practice English *outside* of the classroom.

To help you to be a better learner of English, I have ten "rules" for successful language learning that I encourage you to follow. These rules suggest ways to help you become a successful learner. If you can follow this advice, you too will learn English more successfully. Here are the ten rules.

1. Don't be afraid!

Sometimes we are afraid to speak a foreign language because we think we are going to make terrible mistakes and people will laugh at us. Well, the best learners of foreign languages try not to be afraid. They make a game of learning. They are not anxious about making mistakes. And they sometimes share their fears with friends. You can do that, too, and you will then feel better about yourself.

2. Dive in!

Try to speak out! Try to say things in English! The best way to learn English is to speak it yourself. Don't worry about perfect pronunciation or grammar; other people usually will not criticize you.

3. Believe in yourself.

You have lots of strengths. You have already learned some English. You must believe that you *can* do it! Compliment your fellow learners on their efforts. Then maybe they will return the favor!

4. Develop motivation.

Why are you learning English? Make a list of your reasons for studying English. Those reasons can be your individual goals for this course. If you have your own reasons for learning English, you will have better success.

5. Cooperate with your classmates.

You are learning language in order to communicate with other people. So, practice with other people and you will be more successful. Create your own conversation group outside of class. Try out new ways to communicate in that group. And, in class, remember your classmates are your "team" members, not your opponents.

6. Get the "big" picture!

Sometimes learners look too closely at all the details of language (words, pronunciation, grammar, usage). It's OK to pay attention to those details, but it is also important to understand general meanings (the "big" picture). Maybe you don't know all the right words or grammar, but you can say things anyway. See movies in English. Read books and magazines for pleasure.

7. Don't worry if you're confused.

Learning English is a big task! Sometimes you will feel confused about all the things you have to learn in a foreign language. Try not to worry about everything all at once. Don't try to learn *all* the rules right now. Ask your teacher questions about English. And try to learn a little every day.

8. Trust your "hunches."

Sometimes people think they should analyze everything (grammar rules, word definitions) in their new language. The best learners do some analyzing, but they follow their hunches (their best guesses, their intuitions) about the new language. If they have an intuition that something sounds right, they will try it. So, the next time you feel that something is right, say it. You'll probably be right, and, if you aren't, someone will give you some feedback.

9. Make your mistakes work FOR you.

A mistake is not always "bad." We all make mistakes learning anything new. Successful learners don't worry about mistakes; they learn from them. They take note of their errors and try to correct them the next time. Some things you can do:
- Make a list of your most common mistakes.
- Select grammar points to watch for.
- Tape-record yourself and listen for errors.

10. Set your own goals.

Teachers usually set goals (assignments, homework, classwork) for you. But *you* need to set your own goals, too. You can do that by doing the following:
- Set aside a certain number of hours a week for extra study.
- Learn a certain number of words a day/week.
- Read a certain number of extra pages a day/week.

Take charge of your own learning!

Try to follow at least some of these rules for successful language learning as you work with **A CONVERSATION BOOK 2**. I am sure that you will be a more efficient learner of English, and you will feel proud of your accomplishments. Good luck!

H. Douglas Brown, Ph.D.
American Language Institute
San Francisco State University
San Francisco, CA
May 1997

A CONVERSATION BOOK 2B
English in Everyday Life
Third Edition

WELCOME TO CLASS!

Tell the Class
Write your first name and your last name on the board. • *Tell the class your name.* • *Show your picture to the class.* • *Describe your picture.*

Partner Activity   Partner's Name _____

Introduce yourself to your partner. • *Practice all these ways.*

    A: My name is _____. What's your name? *(or)*
        Hello. I'm _____. What's your name? *(or)*
        Hi. I'm _____. What is your name?

    B: Nice to meet you. My name is _____. *(or)*
        I'm _____. I'm pleased to meet you.

Introduce your partner to the class.

        I'd like you to meet _____. *(or)*
        This is _____.

Group Activity
Work in groups of three or four. • *Write a name tag for yourself.* • *Pronounce the names of each student in your group.* • *Introduce yourself to the others in the group.*

Partner Interview

Partner's Name _____

Practice these questions with your teacher. • Then ask your partner.

1. What is today's date?
2. What is your name?
3. Whereare you from?
4. Where did you study English before?
5. What are your goals for this class?

Write

Write about your partner.

Journal

_____
(1)

My partner's name is _____ (2). My partner is from _____ (3). She/He studied English _____ (4) _____.

His/her goals for this class are _____ (5).

Tell the Class

Read your journal to the class. • Tell the class about your partner.

xxiii

UNIT 1
HOUSING

- 2 Places to Live
- 4 Inside Your Home
- 6 Finding the Right Home
- 8 Utility Problems
- 10 Tenants and Landlords
- 12 Insuring Your Property
- 14 Moving
- 16 Answering the Door
- 18 Neighborhood Problems
- 20 Neighborhood Improvements
- 22 Review

LEARNING STRATEGIES

- ► Check around your neighborhood for homes to rent or buy. How many homes are for rent? How many are for sale?

- ► Find the names of your utility companies on your bills or in your telephone directory. Copy the names and bring them to class. Does everyone in the class have the same utility companies?

- ► Look at your lease agreement. List the words you don't understand. Bring the list to class to discuss.

- ► Interview a family member or friend (outside of class) and find out what they like and don't like about where they live. Write down your findings in the **Activities** section of your notebook.

PLACES TO LIVE

1. congestion
2. countryside
3. farmhouse
4. high-rise
5. housing development
6. land
7. log cabin
8. lot
9. motor home
10. multiple-family dwelling
11. one-story
12. own
13. property
14. ranch house
15. real estate
16. recreational vehicle
17. rental
18. residence
19. semidetached
20. single-family dwelling
21. small town
22. space
23. sprawling
24. suburb
25. tenement
26. town house
27. two-family dwelling
28. two-story
29. village
30. walk-up

See Conversation Springboards on page 98.

Picture Discussion

With your class, answer the questions about the picture story. • Use the vocabulary list. • Add more words.

1. What places to live is this couple looking at? Describe the locations and the types of housing.
2. Which do you think will be most expensive? least expensive? Why?
3. Which property do you think this young couple could buy?
4. What are the advantages and disadvantages of each location? of each type of housing?
5. What other places to live are there? Make lists on the board of locations and types of housing.

What's the Story?

In groups of three, choose a recorder. • Create the young couple's story. • Answer these questions in your story. • Tell your story to another pair of students.

1. Who are they?
2. Where are they from?
3. What do they do for a living?
4. What leisure activities do they enjoy?
5. Where will they decide to live?
6. Why did they come to this area to live?
7. What do they hope to do here?
8. Will they rent or buy their house?

Advantages/Disadvantages

In the same groups, list the advantages and disadvantages of living in a city, a suburb, a small town, and the country. • Read your list to the class. • Make a class list on the board.

Draw with a Partner   Partner's Name _____

With a partner, describe your house or apartment. • From your partner's description, draw a picture of his or her home. • Show the picture to your partner. • Have your partner correct your picture and explain the corrections. • How accurate was your drawing?

INSIDE YOUR HOME

1. cellar
2. convenience
3. cozy
4. cramped
5. customized
6. decorate
7. extra-wide
8. floor covering
9. furnish
10. furnishings
11. handle
12. hang wallpaper
13. mini-blinds
14. modified fixtures
15. occupant
16. privacy
17. redecorate
18. remodel
19. roomy
20. spacious
21. special needs
22. storage space
23. store
24. storeroom
25. wheelchair
26. window treatment

See Conversation Springboards on page 98.

Picture Discussion

With your class, answer the questions about the scenes. • Use the vocabulary list. • Add more words.

1. What are these people doing inside their homes?
2. Where in the building is each apartment located? Where is the laundry room?
3. Describe each room.
4. How will the couple decorate their living room? What furnishings will they have? What floor covering? What window treatment? What will they hang on the walls?
5. Tell the stories of these occupants: Who are they? Where are they from? What are their interests or hobbies?

Group Vocabulary Challenge

In groups of four, list different things people have in their kitchens. • Work fast! • Read your list to the class. • Which group has the longest list? • Make a class list on the board.

Partner Interview   Partner's Name _____

Ask a partner these questions. • Then report your partner's responses to another pair of students.

1. What colors are the walls in your home?
2. What floor coverings are there?
3. What is on the windows?
4. What furniture is in your home? What appliances?
5. What would you like to redecorate? What would you like to change?
6. What would you like to buy for your home?

Class Game: Pantomime

In groups of three, choose a redecorating task. • List instructions for the task. • Pantomime your task for the class. • Have your classmates guess what you are doing. • Read your instructions to the class. • Did you forget anything?

Group Decision

In the same groups, discuss this situation and decide what to do. • Report your decision to the class.

◆ Your apartment is bare. You have $1,000 to spend. Your landlord will supply a stove and refrigerator. What will you buy? How much will you pay for each item?

FINDING THE RIGHT HOME

Apartments for Rent

One-bdrm., 1 bath., fncd. yd., utils. not incl. Call ownr.: 555-1582.

Two-bdrm., 1 bath., kitch. w. dishw., utils. incl., excel. loc., $650/mo.

Studio apt. w. bath., bsmt. laundr. avail., no utils., $450/mo.

Three-bdrm., 2 bath., cpt., ht. and elec. not incl., no pets, $600/mo.

Three-rm. bsmt. apt., furnished, utils. incl., nr. public transp.

Houses for Sale

Condo: 3 rms. w. bath, excel. cond., incl. stove, refrig., dishw., w/w cpt., and more. $65,000.

One-acre fncd. lot w. new mobile home; beautiful view, low dn. pmnt. Asking $47,900.

Two-story, 4 bdrm., 2 bath. Excel. loc., fncd. yd. You'll love it! $125,000, as is.

Family size: *2*
Monthly take-home pay: *$850*

Family size: *6*
Monthly take-home pay: *$1,700*

1. apt. (apartment)
2. as is
3. avail. (available)
4. bath. (bathroom)
5. bdrm. (bedroom)
6. bsmt. (basement)
7. cond. (condition)
8. condo (condominium)
9. cpt. (carpet)
10. dishw. (dishwasher)
11. dn. pmnt. (down payment)
12. elec. (electricity)
13. excel. (excellent)
14. fncd. (fenced)
15. ht. (heat)
16. incl. (included)
17. kitch. (kitchen)
18. laundr. (laundry room)
19. loc. (location)
20. mo. (month)
21. nr. (near)
22. open house
23. ownr. (owner)
24. real estate agent
25. realtor
26. refrig. (refrigerator)
27. rms. (rooms)
28. studio
29. transp. (transportation)
30. utils. (utilities)
31. w. (with)
32. w/w (wall–to–wall)
33. yd. (yard)

See Conversation Springboards on page 98.

Picture Discussion

With your class, answer the questions about the scenes. • Use the vocabulary list. • Add more words.

1. Do you understand these newspaper ads? Read them with your class.
2. Which house is the most expensive? the least expensive?
3. Which is the largest apartment? the smallest apartment?
4. What are the advantages and disadvantages of each apartment or house?
5. What are the special needs of each family?
6. Which home will each family choose?

Group Decision

In groups of three, decide which housing in the newspaper ads is best for each family. • Should they rent or buy? • Report your decisions to another group and explain your reasons. • Did your groups make the same decisions?

Partner Interview   Partner's Name _____

With a partner, ask these questions. • Then report your partner's responses to another pair of students.

1. Which of these housing ads interests you? What do you like about them?
2. Do you prefer a large or a small home? Why?
3. What is your "dream home"? Describe it.
4. Where would it be?
5. Who would live there with you?
6. Would you rent it or buy it? Why?

Group Role Play

In groups of four, write questions to ask a realtor about an apartment or a house. • Then create a role play between a realtor and family. • Have each family member ask the realtor one of your group's questions. • Present your role play to the class.

7

UTILITY PROBLEMS

1. air conditioner
2. blow a fuse
3. blow-dryer
4. current
5. cut off
6. dial tone
7. discontinue
8. extension cord
9. furnace
10. fuse box
11. hot water heater
12. ironing board
13. meter
14. nonpayment
15. notification
16. notify
17. oil heat
18. oil tank
19. overload a circuit
20. plug
21. plug in
22. rewire
23. run out
24. thermostat
25. wiring

8   See Conversation Springboards on pages 98 and 99.

Picture Discussion

With your class, answer the questions about the scenes. • Use the vocabulary list. • Add more words.

1. What is happening in each scene? What utility problems do these two people have?
2. How can they solve their problems?
3. How could these utility problems be avoided?
4. Tell the story of each of these people.

Group Problem Solving

In groups of four, discuss these utility problems. • State the problem. • What advice would you give? • Compare your solution with another group.

◆ You pick up your telephone receiver, but you can't get a dial tone.
◆ There is a bad thunderstorm, and your power is out.
◆ You want to take a hot shower, but the water is cold.

Partner Interview   Partner's Name _____

Ask a partner these questions. • Then report your partner's responses to another pair of students.

1. In your home, what runs on electricity? on gas? on oil?
2. In your home, where are the circuit breakers or fuse boxes? Have you ever changed a fuse or flipped the switch on a circuit breaker?
3. Where are the meters? How do you read them?
4. Have you ever had any problems with utilities? What happened? What did you do?

Cross-Cultural Exchange

In groups of four, choose a conversation monitor and a recorder. • Discuss these questions. • Compare cultures when possible. • Report the results of your discussion to the class.

1. What month is usually the coldest in your hometown? How cold is it (C°? F°?)?
2. What kinds of heating do people have?
3. In what months do people usually have to heat their homes?
4. What month is usually the hottest? How hot is it (C°? F°?)?
5. How do people stay cool in hot weather? Do many people have air conditioning?

TENANTS AND LANDLORDS

1. afford
2. affordable
3. as good as new
4. brand new
5. decent condition
6. fair
7. functional
8. landlady
9. landlord's responsibility
10. leaky
11. maintain
12. maintenance
13. major appliance
14. makeshift
15. melt
16. obligation
17. plumbing
18. serviceable
19. superintendent (super)
20. tenant's rights
21. used
22. working order

See Conversation Springboards on page 99.

Picture Discussion

With your class, answer the questions about the picture story. • Use the vocabulary list. • Add more words.

1. What is happening in each scene? Who are these people? What are they saying to each other?
2. Why doesn't the landlady buy a new refrigerator for the tenant? Why doesn't she buy a new toilet for herself?
3. What responsibilities does the landlady have?
4. What rights does the tenant have?
5. What is the fair thing to do in this situation? Why?
6. How does this story end? Is everyone satisfied with the solution?

Group Problem Solving

In groups of four, discuss these situations. • Find a solution for each problem. • Share your solutions with the class.

Problem 1: The tenants can't pay their rent on time, and the landlord needs the money to fix a broken thermostat.

Problem 2: The tenants want to nail shelves to the apartment walls. The landlord doesn't want nails in the walls.

Problem 3: The tenants are having trouble with their neighbors, so they want to break their lease and move away. The landlord won't let them.

Problem 4: The landlord is raising the rent because property taxes have increased. The tenants cannot afford to pay more rent.

Problem 5: The apartment stairs are broken. The tenants want them fixed. The landlord cannot get a carpenter for six weeks.

Group Role Play

In the same groups, create a role play, illustrating a solution to one of the problems above. • Present your role play to another group.

Cross-Cultural Exchange

In groups of four, choose a conversation monitor and a recorder. • Discuss these questions. • Compare cultures when possible. • Report the results of your discussion to the class.

1. What are tenants' rights in your country? What are landlords' rights?
2. What are tenants' responsibilities? landlords' responsibilities?
3. Who is responsible for cleaning stairways in apartment buildings?
4. Who is responsible for taking the trash outside?
5. Are there limits on the number of people occupying an apartment?
6. Do people hang laundry out of windows to dry?
7. What things do people take outside to clean?
8. Do people wash the sidewalks in front of their homes? How often?
9. Are there restrictions about noise? loud music?

INSURING YOUR PROPERTY

1. assess
2. damage
3. dog bite
4. dwelling
5. fire damage
6. homeowner
7. insurance adjustor
8. insurance coverage
9. liability
10. liable
11. loss of property
12. mandatory insurance
13. optional insurance
14. premium
15. protection
16. repair cost
17. replacement cost
18. smoke damage
19. stolen property
20. storm damage
21. water damage

See Conversation Springboards on page 99.

Picture Discussion

With your class, answer the questions about the scenes. • Use the vocabulary list. • Add more words.

1. What is happening in each scene?
2. What damages or losses do you see in these scenes?
3. What caused the damages or losses?
4. Who are the people? What do you think they are saying?
5. What kind of insurance protection covers each of these situations?

Group Role Play

In groups of three, choose one of the scenes. • Create a role play. • In your role play, explain the situation and discuss the damages or losses and the insurance coverage. • Present your role play to the class.

Group Decision

In the same groups, discuss this scene and decide whether this renter should purchase renter's insurance or not. • If not, think of other ways he can protect his property. • Compare your group's decision with other groups.

Cross-Cultural Exchange

In groups of four, choose a conversation monitor and a recorder. • Discuss these questions. • Compare cultures when possible. • Report the results of your discussion to the class.

1. Do people in your country carry homeowner's or renter's insurance?
2. What kinds of insurance are mandatory? What kinds are optional?
3. How much does insurance usually cost?
4. If people do not have insurance, what do they do when their property is damaged or stolen?

MOVING

1. belongings/possessions
2. breakable
3. bump
4. crate
5. delicate
6. farewell
7. glassware
8. haul
9. household goods
10. leave behind
11. misplace
12. nick
13. organize
14. pack
15. packing box
16. put away
17. transport
18. unload
19. unwrap
20. utility trailer
21. wrap

14   See Conversation Springboards on page 100.

Picture Discussion

With your class, answer the questions about the picture story. • Use the vocabulary list. • Add more words.

1. What is happening in each scene?
2. Did this family have a good experience moving? Why or why not?
3. Was it a good decision for this family to move their own belongings? Why or why not?
4. Why did they move?
5. Do you think they will be happy in their new life?

Group Brainstorm

In groups of four, choose a recorder. • List all the things people do before moving. • Read your list to the class. • Make a class list on the board.

Find Someone Who

Review the vocabulary with your teacher. • Add to this list. • Then interview your classmates and fill in the name of someone who . . .

1. has moved recently. _____
2. has moved many times. _____
3. has helped someone move. _____
4. has lost or broken something in a move. _____
5. hates to move. _____
6. _____ _____
7. _____ _____

Speech

Tell the class about an experience you had while moving. • Was it a good or bad one? • Why?

ANSWERING THE DOOR

1. amazed
2. cautious
3. chain lock
4. charitable
5. charity
6. collection
7. deliver newspapers
8. distrust
9. distrustful
10. door knocker
11. door-to-door
12. fearful
13. Girl Scout
14. lawn mower
15. overgrown
16. pay for
17. special delivery
18. stranger
19. unexpected
20. wary

See Conversation Springboards on page 100.

Picture Discussion

With your class, answer the questions about the scenes. • Use the vocabulary list. • Add more words.

1. What is happening in each scene?
2. How are these people reacting? Why?
3. What are they saying?
4. What will happen next in each scene?

Group Role Play

In groups of three, choose one of the scenes. • Create a role play. • Present your role play to another group.

Group Brainstorm

In groups of four, choose a recorder. • List reasons why people come to your door. • Read your list to the class. • Make a class list on the board.

Group Discussion

In the same groups, choose a recorder. • Discuss these questions. • Compare your answers with another group.

1. Has anyone ever come to your door? Who? What did they want?
2. Do you always open the door? If not, why not? What do you do?
3. What do you say to the people at the door?
4. Do you keep your doors locked? Why or why not?

Partner Activity: Ask Aunt Betty

Partner's Name _____

With a partner, read and discuss this letter. • Together, write a reply from Aunt Betty, *giving advice to* Not His Wife.

ASK AUNT BETTY

Dear Aunt Betty:

We have a problem with our neighbor Matt. My husband and I were friendly with Matt and his wife, Jane. But now Jane has left Matt, and they are getting a divorce.

Ever since Jane left, Matt has come to our door every evening at suppertime. He not only stays for supper but he ends up staying for the whole evening!

I know he is lonely and unhappy, and he likes my home-cooked meals, but I'm getting tired of this. After all, I'm not his wife!

Not His Wife

NEIGHBORHOOD PROBLEMS

1. abandoned	10. hang out	19. run down
2. advocate	11. homeless	20. run over
3. boarded-up	12. inner city	21. stray dog
4. dilapidated	13. junk	22. street light
5. disrepair	14. litter	23. unsafe
6. fire hazard	15. loiter	24. vagrant
7. gang	16. neglect	25. vandal
8. ghetto	17. personal safety	26. vandalism
9. graffiti	18. petition	27. weeds

Picture Discussion

With your class, answer the questions about the scene. • Use vocabulary from the list. • Add more words.

1. Describe this neighborhood.
2. Describe the people in this neighborhood.
3. What are the good things? What are the bad things?
4. What neighborhood improvements is the woman with the petition advocating?
5. Do you think she will be successful? Why or why not?

See Conversation Springboards on page 100.

Group Problem Posing/Problem Solving

In groups of four, list all the problems you see in this neighborhood. • Next to each problem, list a solution. • Share your problems and solutions with the class.

Class Brainstorm

With your class, choose a recorder. • List as many neighborhood problems as possible. • Next to each problem, list a solution.

Find Someone Who

Review the vocabulary with your teacher. • Add to this list. • Then interview your classmates and fill in the name of someone who . . .

1. lives in a quiet neighborhood. _____

2. lives in a neighborhood with heavy traffic. _____

3. has parking problems in the neighborhood. _____

4. worries about personal safety in the neighborhood. _____

5. _____ _____

6. _____ _____

Community Activity

With your class, add to this list of housing problems. • Check the problems that apply to your community. • Find out what your community is doing to solve these problems. • Report the results to the class.

☐ not enough housing   ☐ _____

☐ housing too expensive   ☐ _____

☐ housing in poor condition   ☐ _____

☐ inadequate water and sewage ☐ _____

NEIGHBORHOOD IMPROVEMENTS

1. alternate-side parking
2. clean-up campaign
3. crime watch
4. friendliness
5. grass-roots organization
6. help out
7. leash law
8. neighborhood association
9. neighborly
10. occupied
11. off-street parking
12. optimism
13. outlook
14. pitch in
15. rainbow
16. refurbish
17. rehabilitate
18. rehabilitation
19. renovate
20. renovation
21. sober
22. urban renewal

Picture Discussion

With your class, answer the questions about the scene. • Use the vocabulary list. • Add more words.

1. What changes have taken place in this neighborhood?
2. What are the people doing? How have they changed?
3. What are the improvements in neighborhood safety? neighbors' attitudes? property maintenance?
4. What does it mean to be neighborly? What neighborly actions are in this scene?
5. Why are grass-roots organizations important?

See Conversation Springboards on pages 100 and 101.

Group Survey

In groups of four, complete this survey. • Report your results to the class.

1. Who lives in the noisiest neighborhood? the quietest neighborhood?
2. Who lives in the cleanest neighborhood? the dirtiest neighborhood?
3. Whose neighborhood is the safest? the most dangerous?
4. Whose neighborhood has the most parking problems? the fewest?
5. Whose neighborhood has the most children? the fewest?
6. Who likes his or her neighborhood the most? Why?
7. Who likes his or her neighborhood the least? Why?
8. What is the worst neighborhood problem? What do the neighbors do about the problem?

Cross-Cultural Exchange

In the same groups, choose a conversation monitor and a recorder. • Discuss these questions. • Compare cultures when possible. • Report the results of your discussion to the class.

1. What makes a neighborhood "good" in your culture? Describe a "good neighborhood."
2. What makes a neighbor "good" in your culture?
3. Describe a person you know who is a good neighbor. What has this person done that is neighborly?
4. What was your neighborhood like in your hometown?

Group Brainstorm

In groups of three, choose a recorder. • List ways to be neighborly. • Include things to do and things to say. • Read your list to the class. • Make a class list on the board. • How many different ways to be neighborly did your class think of?

Group Role Play

In the same groups, choose one way to be neighborly from your list. • Create a role play. • Present your role play to another group.

Community Activity

Discuss these questions with your class. • Decide how you will find answers to them. • Where can you look? • Whom can you ask? • In groups of four, find the answers and report back to the class.

1. Are there groups that are actively working to make improvements in your community? What are they?
2. What improvements are they making right now?
3. What improvements would you like to see in your community?

21

REVIEW

Partner Game: *What Do You Remember?*   Partner's Name _____

With a partner, look at the scenes of the neighborhood in Neighborhood Problems and Neighborhood Improvements on pages 18 and 20. • Remember as much as you can. • Close your books. • Describe the differences with your partner. • List everything. • Compare your list with another pair. • Add to your lists. • Open the book and look at the scenes. • What did you forget?

Group Questions

In groups of four, write questions that are important to ask before renting an apartment. • Compare your group's list with another group.

Partner Interview   Partner's Name _____

With a partner, write eight questions to ask about your home and neighborhood. • Ask another pair the questions. • Then report your questions and answers to another group of students.

Draw with a Partner   Partner's Name _____

Draw your dream home. • Describe it to a partner. • Then describe your partner's dream home to another pair of students.

Group Problem Posing

In groups of four, list problems people have with neighbors, neighborhoods, landlords, and tenants. • Compare your group's list with another group.

Group Role Play

In the same groups, choose one of the problems you listed. • Create a problem-solving role play. • Present your role play to the class.

UNIT 2
TRANSPORTATION AND TRAVEL

24 Commuting
26 Learning to Drive
28 Driving Problems
30 Buying a Car
32 On Vacation
34 Traveling by Car
36 Bus and Train Travel
38 Air Travel
40 Review

LEARNING STRATEGIES

➤ Find written information about your local area. Create a class file and bulletin board with brochures, maps, and posters of different local tourist attractions.

➤ Write a letter to a friend coming to visit. Tell your friend about some of your favorite local sights.

➤ Look for good travel deals in advertisements. Bring them to class. Create a bulletin board of travel ads and interesting places to visit.

➤ Tell someone about your ideal vacation trip. Ask them what theirs is and compare your opinions.

COMMUTING

1. accessible
2. bumper-to-bumper
3. bus shelter
4. car pool
5. carpool
6. car pool lane
7. commuter
8. daily commute
9. detour
10. direct
11. gridlock
12. heavy traffic
13. kneeling bus
14. motorist
15. passing lane
16. restricted lane
17. road crew
18. road repair
19. route map
20. rush hour
21. signal
22. stuck in traffic
23. time-consuming
24. timesaving
25. traffic jam/ tie-up
26. under construction
27. wheelchair access

Picture Discussion

With your class, answer the questions about the scenes. • Use the vocabulary list. • Add more words.

1. What are these bus commuters doing?
2. What other things do commuters sometimes do on a bus? What do they do while they're waiting for a bus?
3. How will the man in the wheelchair get on the bus?
4. When can motorists use the carpool lane for carpooling?
5. Why is carpooling a good idea?
6. Why do the cars have to detour?
7. What other reasons are there for detours? for traffic tie-ups?
8. What are the advantages of taking a bus or train to work? What are the disadvantages?
9. What are the advantages and disadvantages of carpooling?

See Conversation Springboards on page 101.

Partner Interview   Partner's Name _____

Ask a partner these questions. • Then report your partner's responses to another pair of students.

1. How do you come to school?
2. How far do you live from school?
3. How long does it take you to get to school?
4. Are there other ways to travel to school? What are they?
5. How do you get to work? Is your commute easy?
6. How long does it take you to get to work?

Community Activity

In groups of four, list every way to commute in your community. • Write the telephone numbers of the transportation companies. • Call and find out the cost of each. • Which is most convenient for you? • Why?

Dialog Journal   Partner's Name _____

*Write a **Journal** entry about an experience you have had commuting to school or work. • Then read your entry to a partner. • Ask questions about your partner's entry.*

25

LEARNING TO DRIVE

1. back in
2. back up
3. curb
4. driver education
5. driving instructor
6. driving manual
7. experienced
8. fail
9. inexperienced
10. issue
11. knock over
12. motor vehicle bureau (MVB)
13. parallel park
14. pass
15. renew
16. retake
17. reverse
18. road test
19. steer
20. traffic cone/pylon
21. vision test
22. written test

26   See Conversation Springboards on page 101.

Picture Discussion

With your class, answer the questions about the picture story. • Use the vocabulary list. • Add more words.

1. What class is in the first scene? What is the textbook? What is the instructor saying?
2. What tests are required for a driver license?
3. Which test does the young man fail? Why does he fail?
4. What does he do after he fails? Why is he finally smiling?
5. How will he become an experienced driver?
6. What test will he need to take again to renew his license.
7. Tell the story of this young man's experience learning to drive.

Group Discussion

In groups of four, choose a recorder. • Answer these questions. • Then report your information to another group. • Share the most interesting facts with the class.

1. Do you have a driver license? Where was it issued?
2. What was the fee for your license?
3. Does your license have restrictions? What are they?
4. Where in your community can you apply for or renew a driver license? Can you renew by mail?
5. What other related services are offered at the same office?
6. Do you have an international driver license? Where have you used it?

Conversation Squares

In groups of three, fill in the chart. • First write your own answers. • Then ask your partners the questions and write their answers. • Compare your group's answers with another group.

	You	Partner 1	Partner 2
Student's Name			
When was the first time you drove?			
Who taught you?			
Did you have any problems learning to drive?			
Did you pass the test the first time?			

Share Your Story

In the same groups, tell about your experience while learning to drive. • Decide which story to tell the class.

DRIVING PROBLEMS

1. accident report
2. blood alcohol level
3. Breathalyzer test
4. change a tire
5. collide
6. collision
7. dent
8. driving under the influence
9. drunk driving
10. emission
11. exhaust
12. fender bender
13. flat tire
14. intoxicated
15. intoxication
16. jack
17. jack up
18. lugnut
19. lug wrench
20. minor accident
21. no-fault/ liability insurance
22. spare tire
23. tail pipe
24. ticket
25. violate
26. violation

28 See Conversation Springboards on page 102.

Picture Discussion

With your class, answer the questions about the scenes. • Use the vocabulary list. • Add more words.

1. How did the woman get a flat tire? What does she need to do to change her tire?
2. Why did the accident happen? Whose fault was it?
3. What will happen to the intoxicated driver?
4. What will the driver of the other car have to do about the accident?
5. What problems does the man's car have? What will he have to do?
6. What is each police officer doing?

Partner Role Play   Partner's Name _____

With a partner, create thought balloons for each scene. • Compare your balloons with another pair. • Choose one of the scenes and create a role play. • Present your role play to the class.

What Do You Say? What Do You Do?

In groups of four, state the problem. • Decide what to say and do in each situation. • Compare your decisions with the class.

1. Your insurance expired and you forgot to renew it.
2. You are driving down the highway and you hit a dog that runs into the road.
3. You are driving down the street and you notice the car in front of you is losing its tail pipe.
4. A police officer has stopped you for speeding. You are rushing to get home because your mother is very ill.

Cross-Cultural Exchange

In the same groups, choose a conversation monitor and a recorder. • Discuss these questions. • Compare cultures when possible. • Report the results of your discussion to the class.

1. In your country, what kinds of cars are popular?
2. Is insurance required?
3. What happens when there is a minor accident?
4. What happens when a police officer stops someone for driving while intoxicated?
5. What are the most common driving problems in your country?

Community Activity

*In the same groups, bring in an automobile insurance policy. • Discuss the insurance coverage. • Decide what coverage is best. • List the new vocabulary on the board. • Copy the new words in the **Vocabulary** section of your notebook.*

BUYING A CAR

1. add-on
2. bad deal
3. bucket seats
4. car dealer
5. compact car
6. economical
7. economy car
8. 4 × 4
9. four-door
10. good deal
11. make
12. make a deal
13. model
14. negotiable
15. negotiate
16. option
17. optional
18. roof rack
19. sales pitch
20. sedan
21. showroom
22. sports utility vehicle
23. station wagon
24. sticker price
25. sun roof
26. truth in advertising
27. two-door
28. used car lot
29. van

30   See Conversation Springboards on page 102.

Picture Discussion

With your class, answer the questions about the scenes. • Use the vocabulary list. • Add more words.

1. What kinds of vehicles are for sale in these scenes?
2. What makes and models do they look like?
3. What are the advantages and disadvantages of each deal?
4. Which car looks like the best deal? Why?
5. What questions should these people ask about each car?

Partner Role Play   Partner's Name _____

With a partner, create a role play about one of the ads. • Present your role play to the class.

Group Brainstorm

In groups of three, choose a recorder. • List options found in a car or other vehicle. • Read your list to the class. • Make a class list on the board.

Community Activity

In groups of four, bring in car ads from the newspaper. • Read them together. • List the abbreviations on the board and discuss them. • Choose a car you would like to buy. • Tell the class about the car and why you chose it.

ON VACATION

1. beach house	9. mountain bike	16. snowcapped
2. bungalow	10. mountain climbing	17. travel agent
3. castle		18. traveler
4. exotic	11. package tour	19. vacationer
5. faraway places	12. rental car	20. view
6. hammock	13. scenery	21. vista
7. hike	14. scenic	22. youth hostel
8. hiker	15. sea	

Picture Discussion

With your class, answer the questions about the scenes. • Use the vocabulary list. • Add more words.

1. Where are the students dreaming of going on vacation?
2. Where will they stay? What will they do?
3. How long will each vacation last?
4. What kind of preparations does each student have to make for the vacation?
5. How much will each vacation cost?
6. Which vacation would you enjoy most? least? Why?

See Conversation Springboards on page 102.

Partner Role Play

Partner's Name _____

With a partner, decide on a place to go for a vacation. • Create a role play between a traveler and a travel agent. • Present your role play to the class.

Partner Activity: Ask Aunt Betty

Partner's Name _____

With the same partner, read and discuss this letter. • Together, write a response from Aunt Betty, giving advice to Illegal in Illinois. • Read your letter to the class.

ASK AUNT BETTY

Dear Aunt Betty:

I am planning to visit my family in my home country. I'm not sure how to do this because I am living in this country illegally. I meant to renew my student visa, but since I was busy working and going to school, I forgot.

Now it's my grandmother's birthday, and my family wants me to come home. What should I do?

Illegal in Illinois

Share Your Story

In groups of four, tell about the best or worst vacation you have ever had. • Decide which story to tell the class.

Community Activity

Choose a place you would like to visit. • Go to a travel agent and get brochures and information. • Tell the class what you learned.

TRAVELING BY CAR

1. access road
2. back seat
3. barrier
4. billboard
5. exact change lane
6. expressway/ freeway
7. family reunion
8. fill up
9. full-service station
10. highway
11. highway patrol
12. interstate
13. main road
14. night clerk
15. pump gas
16. registration desk/front desk
17. rest stop
18. roadkill
19. road trip
20. roadside motel
21. shoulder
22. speeding ticket
23. station attendant
24. toll
25. toll booth
26. toll road
27. turnpike

34 See Conversation Springboards on page 103.

Picture Discussion

With your class, answer the questions about the picture story. • Use the vocabulary list. • Add more words.

1. What is the family doing in this story?
2. Where are they going?
3. How many miles do you think they have to travel?
4. What time do they leave? How many days does the trip take? What time do they arrive?
5. How fast do they drive?
6. What might they do at rest stops along the way?
7. What is the highway patrol officer doing?
8. What do the adults do in the car? What do the children do? What does the dog do?

Advantages/Disadvantages

In groups of three, discuss the advantages and disadvantages of traveling by car. • Share your information with another group. • Report the most interesting ideas to the class.

What Do You Say? What Do You Do?

In the same groups, state the problem. • Decide what to say and do in each situation. • Compare your decisions with the class.

1. You need directions to get to the main highway.
2. You don't know how much the toll is.
3. You don't know where the nearest gas station is.
4. You are driving on a highway and are completely lost.

Cross-Cultural Exchange

In groups of five, choose a conversation monitor and a recorder. • Discuss these questions. • Compare cultures when possible. • Report the results of your discussion to the class.

1. In your country, do people take long road trips? Where to?
2. What are the speed limits on highways in your country?
3. Are there toll roads? How much are the tolls?
4. Are there rest stops? What are they like?

BUS AND TRAIN TRAVEL

1. arrive
2. board
3. bus station
4. coach
5. conductor
6. depart
7. destination
8. dining car
9. distressed
10. inform
11. information board
12. information booth
13. locomotive
14. porter
15. sleeper car
16. terminal
17. ticket agent
18. ticket counter
19. time change
20. time zone
21. train platform
22. train station
23. waiting area

Picture Discussion

With your class, answer the questions about the scenes. • Use the vocabulary list. • Add more words.

1. What are all the people doing in each scene? What are their destinations?
2. What is the ticketing agent at the bus station ticket counter saying to the young man?
3. Why does the train station have three clocks showing different times?
4. Why is the man at the train station information booth so distressed? What is he shouting? What will the agent at the booth do to help him?
5. What is similar about bus travel and train travel? What is different? What are the advantages and disadvantages of each?

See Conversation Springboards on page 103.

What's the Story?

In groups of four, choose a recorder. • Tell a story about one of these travelers. • Where is the traveler going? • Why? • Everyone in the group should contribute at least two sentences. • Read your story to the class.

What Do You Say? What Do You Do?

In the same groups, decide what to say and do in each situation. • Compare your decisions with the class.

1. Your friend is arriving on the 8:12 train from Boston. It's 8:30 and the train hasn't arrived.
2. You need information about taking a bus from Dallas to Los Angeles. Find out the departure times and the prices.
3. You are waiting in line at the bus station. The person in front of you is trying to buy a one-way ticket to New York, but he doesn't speak English very well—he speaks your first language. Try to assist him.

Group Brainstorm

In the same groups, choose a recorder. • List questions travelers ask at an information booth in a bus or train station. • Read your list to the class. • Make a class list on the board.

Partner Interview

Partner's Name _____

Ask a partner these questions. • Then report your partner's responses to another pair of students.

1. When was the last time you traveled by bus or train?
2. Where did you go?
3. What was the fare?
4. How long did the trip take?
5. Describe the trip: Was the bus or train crowded? Were you able to get a seat? Where did you sit? What did you do? Who else was traveling with you?

AIR TRAVEL

1. aisle seat
2. baggage carousel
3. baggage cart
4. baggage claim
5. boarding pass
6. carry-on bag
7. check baggage
8. check-in counter
9. claim check
10. customs
11. customs declaration form
12. disembarkation card
13. embarkation card
14. flight attendant
15. gate
16. immigration
17. in-flight meal
18. metal detector
19. overhead compartment
20. security check
21. special meal
22. ticket stub
23. tilt
24. tray
25. tray table
26. upright position
27. window seat

See Conversation Springboards on page 103.

Picture Discussion

With your class, answer the questions about the picture story. • Use the vocabulary list. • Add more words.

1. What is happening in each scene?
2. What are the airport procedures for departure? for arrival?
3. What procedures are different for international travel?
4. Tell the story of this young man's trip.

Partner Role Play   Partner's Name _____

You are at the airport, checking in for an international flight. • With a partner, create a role play between the passenger and the ticket agent. • Present your role play to the class.

What Do You Say? What Do You Do?

In groups of four, state the problem. • Decide what to say and do in each situation. • Compare your decisions with the class.

1. You go through the security check, and the buckle on your belt sets off the alarm.
2. You are on an airplane, and a little girl behind you is kicking the seat.
3. You are on an airplane and you don't feel very well.
4. After you leave the terminal with one suitcase, you remember you left a bag on the carousel.

Community Activity

In the same groups, research these questions. • Report your findings to the class.

1. Where can you apply for a passport in your community?
2. Where can you get travel information in your community?
3. What is the closest airport? How long does it take to get there from your home? from the school? Is there public transportation to the airport?

REVIEW

Group Vocabulary Challenge

In groups of four, list as many types of transportation as you can. • Work fast! • Read your list to the class. • Which group has the longest list? • Make a class list on the board.

Draw with a Partner   Partner's Name _____

What kind of car would you like to have? • Draw a picture. • Then list all the features you would like. • Explain your dream car to a partner. • How much does it cost? • Find an ad in the newspaper that comes the closest to your dream car.

Partner Questions   Partner's Name _____

With a partner, write five questions about traveling. • Then ask your questions to another pair of students. • Present your questions and answers to the class.

Partner Activity: Ask Aunt Betty   Partner's Name _____

With a partner, write to Aunt Betty, asking for advice about a transportation problem. • Then exchange with another pair. • Respond to their letter. • Read their letter and your reply to the class.

Partner Game: What Do You Remember?

Partner's Name _____

With a partner, look at one of the stories or scenes in this unit. • Remember as much as you can. • Close your books. • Describe the scene with your partner. • List everything. • Which pair of students has the longest list in the class?

Partner Lists   Partner's Name _____

With a partner, list as many driving and commuting problems as you can. • Compare lists with your classmates. • Who has the longest list? • Choose three problems from your list. • Find solutions with your partner. • Read your solutions to another pair.

40

UNIT 3
FINDING A JOB

- 42 Jobs in Your Community
- 46 Your Occupation
- 48 The Right Job for You
- 50 Looking for a Job
- 52 Applying for a Job
- 54 Wages and Benefits
- 56 Review

LEARNING STRATEGIES

- In the **Vocabulary** section of your notebook, list the jobs you see people doing every day and the skills required for each job.
- Watch the news and commercials on TV every day. Add to your list the different jobs you see.
- Do you have questions about your list? Ask your family, friends, teacher, and classmates about the jobs on your list.
- Write about your list in the **Journal** section of your notebook. Divide your list into jobs you think you would like and jobs you think you would not like. Explain your reasons.

JOBS IN YOUR COMMUNITY

1. agriculture
2. arts
3. banking
4. beauty care
5. commerce
6. communications
7. design
8. entertainment
9. food service
10. government
11. health care industry
12. industry
13. law enforcement
14. manufacturing
15. money management
16. news media
17. occupation
18. office work
19. photography
20. private sector
21. public service
22. retail sales
23. security
24. service industry
25. shipping
26. tourism
27. vendor

42   See Conversation Springboards on page 104.

Picture Discussion

With your class, answer the questions about the scenes. • Use the vocabulary list. • Add more words.

1. What kinds of workers do the students see in these scenes? Make a list on the board.
2. Describe the job each person does.
3. What general occupation does each worker fit into?
4. What other kinds of jobs fit into these occupations?

Group Brainstorm

In groups of four, choose a recorder. • Fill in the five charts with answers to the questions. • Report your information to the class.

1. What fruits, vegetables, trees, and flowers are grown in your community? What jobs in agriculture are available there?

Agriculture	Jobs

2. What industries are in your community? What large companies? What kinds of jobs are available there?

Industries/Large Companies	Jobs

3. What small businesses are in your community? What kinds of jobs are available there?

Small Businesses	Jobs

4. What places in your community provide food services? What food service jobs are available there?

Places with Food Services	Jobs
_____	_____
_____	_____
_____	_____
_____	_____

5. What other kinds of services are provided in your community? What service-related jobs are there?

Other Services	Jobs
_____	_____
_____	_____
_____	_____
_____	_____

Cross-Cultural Exchange

In the same groups, choose a conversation monitor and a recorder. • Discuss these questions. • Compare cultures when possible. • Report the results of your discussion to the class.

1. What businesses and industries are in your hometown?
2. What jobs are most common there?
3. What are the wages?
4. What is the training necessary for each job?

Class Interview

Who has a job in your community? • With your class, write a list of questions on the board about the different jobs people have. • Conduct class interviews with them. • Interview your teacher first!

Community Activity

In groups of three, choose a place in your community to research. • Go there, and list all the workplaces, workers, kinds of work, and occupation categories you see. • Report your findings to the class.

YOUR OCCUPATION

1. administrative assistant
2. auto worker
3. blue collar
4. certification
5. clerical
6. executive
7. first shift
8. hospital worker
9. inspector
10. management
11. night shift
12. office worker
13. overtime
14. second shift
15. secretarial
16. self-employed
17. shift
18. third shift
19. underemployed
20. unqualified
21. white collar

See Conversation Springboards on page 104.

Picture Discussion

With your class, answer the questions about the scenes. • Use the vocabulary list. • Add more words.

1. What is happening in each scene?
2. What occupations do these students have?
3. What shift does each person work?
4. What kind of preparation did each student need for his or her occupation?
5. The hospital aide was a doctor in her country. Why is she underemployed?
6. Do any of these jobs require certification? What other jobs require certification?
7. Which of these occupations are hazardous? Why?
8. Are these people happy with their occupations? Why or why not?

Group Vocabulary Challenge

*In groups of four, list as many occupations as you can. • Work fast! • Read your list to the class. • Which group has the longest list? • Make a class list on the board. • Copy the new words in the **Vocabulary** section of your notebook.*

Group Brainstorm

In the same groups, choose a recorder. • List questions to ask about someone's job. • Read your list to the class. • Make a class list on the board.

Class Survey

With your class, add to this list of questions. • Interview your classmates. • Report your results to the class. • How many members of your class . . .

1. have worked full time? _____
2. have worked part time? _____
3. have been unemployed? _____
4. have worked overtime? _____
5. have worked the first shift? _____
6. have worked the night shift? _____
7. have been self-employed? _____
8. have been underemployed? _____
9. _____ _____
10. _____ _____

Speech

Present a two-minute speech to your class about your job or occupation. • Use notecards, but do not read your speech. • Practice your speech with a partner first.

THE RIGHT JOB FOR YOU

1. analytical
2. analyze
3. build
4. builder
5. challenge
6. challenging
7. construction site
8. coordinate
9. elementary school teacher
10. heavy equipment operator
11. independent
12. interesting
13. job training
14. manual labor
15. medical technician
16. men's apparel/fashion
17. paraprofessional
18. presentation
19. professional
20. skilled
21. solve problems
22. technical
23. unskilled
24. work environment

Picture Discussion

With your class, answer the questions about the scenes. • Use the vocabulary list. • Add more words.

1. What jobs is this student imagining?
2. What work would he do in each job?
3. What would he wear for each job?
4. What would be the advantages of each job?
5. What would be the disadvantages of each job?

48   See Conversation Springboards on pages 104 and 105.

Draw with a Partner   Partner's Name _____

With a partner, fill in the empty bubble with one more job possibility. • Decide which job the student should choose. • Explain your decision to another pair.

Partner Interview   Partner's Name _____

With a partner, ask the questions on this Job Interest Inventory Survey about job preferences. • Then report your partner's responses to another pair.

JOB INTEREST INVENTORY SURVEY

1. Which are more important to you in a job?
   - ☐ friendly co-workers   ☐ convenient location   ☐ other: _____
   - ☐ a good supervisor   ☐ interesting work
   - ☐ good pay   ☐ chance for advancement
   - ☐ convenient hours   ☐ challenging work

   Explain your answer: _____

2. Do you prefer to work quickly or slowly? Explain your answer:

   _____

3. Which are important in your work environment?
   - ☐ noise level   ☐ temperature   ☐ lighting   ☐ other: _____
   - ☐ odors   ☐ space   ☐ indoors/outdoors

   Explain your answer: _____

4. Are you willing to travel? to live in another country? Explain your answer:

   _____

5. Which of these do you like to do?
   - ☐ make things   ☐ perform or make presentations
   - ☐ help people   ☐ solve problems
   - ☐ buy or sell things   ☐ other: _____

   Explain your answer: _____

6. How much preparation or training time are you willing to spend?
   - ☐ a few weeks   ☐ six months
   - ☐ two years   ☐ four years
   - ☐ six years   ☐ other: _____

   Explain your answer: _____

7. What is your ideal job?
   Explain your answer: _____

LOOKING FOR A JOB

1. bulletin board
2. classified advertisement (ad)
3. employment agency
4. employment counselor
5. entry level
6. experience necessary
7. help wanted sign
8. inquire
9. job lead
10. job qualification
11. job search
12. make an inquiry
13. no experience required
14. position
15. post
16. recommend
17. recommendation
18. seek employment
19. telephone interview
20. word of mouth

Picture Discussion

With your class, answer the questions about the picture story. • Use the vocabulary list. • Add more words.

1. What is happening in the story?
2. What are the people saying in each scene?
3. What different methods is this man using to look for a job?
4. What other methods could he use to find a job?

See Conversation Springboards on page 105.

Partner Role Play

Partner's Name _____

With a partner, choose one of the scenes. • Create a role play. • Present your role play to another pair of students.

Find Someone Who

Review the vocabulary with your teacher. • Add to this list. • Then ask your classmates and fill in the name of someone who . . .

1. has found a job from a newspaper ad. _____

2. has found a job through an employment agency. _____

3. has found a job through a HELP WANTED sign in a window. _____

4. has found a job through a friend. _____

5. is looking for a job now. _____

6. _____ _____

7. _____ _____

Group Decision

In groups of four, read the employment opportunities listed in this sample newspaper classified section.

◆ Discuss the abilities, experience, and job needs of each member of your group.
◆ Discuss the advantages and disadvantages of each job.
◆ Do any of these jobs appeal to anyone in your group?
◆ Choose the best job for each member of your group.
◆ If there is no appropriate job listed, write one.
◆ Report your decisions to the class.

CLASSIFIED/HELP WAN

DOUG'S DELIVERY IS LOOKING FOR friendly, courteous, and effective customer service representatives and meal couriers. Call 555-2173 for details.

HAIRDRESSER
Immediate opening for colorist/stylist for upscale French salon/treatment center. No following necessary. To apply, fax resume to Béatrice at 555-6252.

MANAGEMENT TRAINEE
Entry-level position available with Arizona branch of nation's leading motor carrier. Applicant must be willing to work all shifts in fast-paced environment. College degree preferred. Send resume to: T6400 Tribune 85890

OFFICE MANAGER
Bright, energetic & take-charge person needed by a downtown giftware co. Resume to: T5411 Daily Star 10024

PEST CONTROL TECHNICIAN needed. Apply at Pacific Pest Control, 34 S. 8th St., M-F 9am-1pm.

PHOTOGRAPHER'S ASSISTANT
Will train; must be energetic, friendly, outgoing. Apply in person: Jake's Old Time Photo, 24th and Adams, Millville.

SALES
PERSONALITY PLUS
Co. in growth stage seeking 2 key people; above-average attitude; neat appearance a must. Call 555-2316. Training available.

SECRETARY/RECEPTIONIST
Prefer. exp. in construction industry, Woodbury location. Computer skills required. Busy office. Fax resume: 555-7655.

STEP AEROBICS INSTRUCTOR
Certification required. Sierra Athletic Club, Sierra, 555-1398.

SUPERINTENDENT
Wanted with exp. & tools. Interviews to be held this week betw. 10am & 1pm at 22 92nd St., Newtown, 555-8342. Call for directions only.

51

APPLYING FOR A JOB

1. applicant
2. availability
3. career objective
4. contact
5. director
6. first impression
7. hire
8. human resources
9. interview
10. interviewer
11. job application
12. job offer
13. job reference
14. minimum wage
15. personnel department
16. position desired
17. proper appearance
18. punctual
19. recruit
20. recruiter
21. recruitment
22. requirement
23. resume
24. starting salary
25. well qualified
26. work history

Picture Discussion

With your class, answer the questions about the picture story. • Use the vocabulary list. • Add more words.

1. What is happening in each scene? What are the people saying?
2. What is each applicant wearing? Are the clothes appropriate? Why or why not?
3. What information does the job application ask for?
4. What information would be on each applicant's resume?
5. How does each applicant feel about this interview?
6. How does the personnel director feel about each applicant?

See Conversation Springboards on page 105.

What's the Story?

In groups of three, tell the story of one of these job applicants. • Report your story to the class. • Answer these questions.

1. What job is the person applying for?
2. What is the starting salary?
3. What is the person's work history? What special skills does he or she have?
4. Does he or she get the job? Why?

Group Discussion

In groups of four, discuss these questions. • Use the words from the vocabulary list. • Then report your information to the class.

1. Should you include all of your work history on a job application? Explain your answer.
2. What should you do if you cannot arrive on time for your interview?
3. What should you wear to an interview?
4. What would you do if the interviewer said the company could not meet your salary requirements?
5. What would you say if the interviewer tells you that the company cannot give you the job you want?
6. What could you list as special skills, awards, training certifications, or other abilities?
7. Who would you use as a job reference? Why?

Group Questions

In groups of four, list two sets of job interview questions: (1) questions the interviewer will ask and (2) questions the applicant should ask. • Read your questions to the class. • Make a class list of the two sets of questions.

Partner Role Play   Partner's Name _____

With a partner, create a role play of a job interview. • Use your group interview questions from above. • Present your role play to another pair.

53

WAGES AND BENEFITS

1. accidental death and dismemberment insurance (AD&D)
2. annual
3. benefits package
4. bimonthly
5. biweekly
6. bonus
7. child care
8. commission
9. compensation
10. contract
11. dental coverage
12. dependent coverage
13. early retirement
14. group insurance
15. income
16. insurance policy
17. insurance premium
18. leave of absence
19. life insurance
20. medical coverage
21. monthly
22. paid vacation
23. profit sharing
24. reimburse
25. reimbursement
26. remuneration
27. salary
28. savings plan
29. unpaid leave

See Conversation Springboards on page 106.

Picture Discussion

With your class, answer the questions about the scenes. • Use the vocabulary list. • Add more words.

1. What benefit does each scene illustrate? Describe each one.
2. What other benefits are there? Fill in the empty bubble with one example.
3. What forms is the new employee signing?
4. Who is he talking to?
5. What are some reasons to take a leave of absence?
6. Why is life insurance important?
7. What are some advantages of early retirement?

Group Decision

In groups of three, decide which one of these jobs you would choose. • In each job, the work is exactly the same. • The only differences are the wages, hours, benefits, and commute. • Report your decision and reasons to the class.

Job 1: Pays $14 per hour. Part-time job. At least 15 hours per week guaranteed, with possibly up to 40 hours some weeks. No benefits. Fifteen-minute walk.

Job 2: Pays $8 per hour, plus time-and-a-half for overtime. Full-time job, 40 hours per week. Benefits package includes health, one-week paid vacation plus four paid holidays, and child care available on site. Half-hour commute by car; no public transportation.

Job 3: Pays $10 per hour. Full-time job, 40 hours per week. Complete benefits package includes health and life insurance, two-week paid vacation plus five paid holidays, and company retirement plan. No child care. One-hour commute by train.

Group Brainstorm

In the same groups, choose a recorder. • List reasons to ask for a raise. • Read your list to the class. • Make a class list on the board. • Which are the best reasons?

Community Activity

Bring a local newspaper to class. • With a partner, list the best jobs, wages, and benefits from the Help Wanted section. • Report your list to the class. • Make a class list on the board. • What jobs are available? • How much do they pay? • What benefits are offered?

Cross-Cultural Exchange

In groups of four, choose a conversation monitor and a recorder. • Discuss these questions. • Compare cultures when possible. • Report the results of your discussion to the class.

1. What job benefits are common in your country? Describe them.
2. What benefits do people have when they lose their job?
3. What are the best paying jobs?
4. Which jobs are the most secure?

REVIEW

Partner Game: *What Do You Remember?*   Partner's Name _____

With a partner, make four lists about jobs in your community. • Include as many items as you can remember. • Compare your lists with another pair.

Places Where People Work	Jobs People Have	Ways to Find a Job	Job Benefits
_____	_____	_____	_____
_____	_____	_____	_____
_____	_____	_____	_____
_____	_____	_____	_____
_____	_____	_____	_____
_____	_____	_____	_____
_____	_____	_____	_____
_____	_____	_____	_____

Partner Interview   Partner's Name _____

With a partner, ask these questions. • Then report your partner's responses to another pair of students.

1. What different kinds of jobs have you had? Describe them.
2. Which job did you like best? What did you like about it?
3. How did you find that job?
4. What kind of job would you like to have? What appeals to you about that job?
5. What preparation will you need for that job?
6. How long will the preparation take?
7. What is most important to you in a job?

Partner Role Play   Partner's Name _____

With a partner, write five good questions for an interviewer to ask in a job interview. • Write five good questions for the job applicant to ask. • Create a role play for a job interview with these questions. • Present your role play to the class.

Group Brainstorm

In groups of four, choose a recorder. • List some good advice for someone who is looking for a job. • Report your advice to the class.

UNIT 4
LIFE AT WORK

- 58 Starting a New Job
- 60 Instructions at Work
- 62 Doing a Good Job
- 64 Injuries at Work
- 66 Deductions from Pay
- 68 Spending Money
- 70 Paying Taxes
- 72 Leaving a Job
- 74 Review

LEARNING STRATEGIES

- ➤ In the **Journal** section of your notebook, write an entry about all the skills you have. Write a second entry about all the skills you would like to have and why you would like to have them.

- ➤ Listen carefully to what people say as they do their work in everyday life. Also, watch and listen carefully to TV programs that involve people at work. Take notes in the **Vocabulary** section of your notebook. Report your findings to the class.

- ➤ Visit a place where people are working. Notice if people are doing a good job or bad job. Notice their attitude, too. Report your findings to the class.

STARTING A NEW JOB

1. anxiety
2. anxious
3. awkward
4. colleague
5. complicated
6. eager
7. embarrassed
8. enthusiasm
9. enthusiastic
10. haste
11. hasty
12. impatience
13. intimidate
14. intimidating
15. knowledgeable
16. lunch break
17. mistake
18. paper jam
19. probationary period
20. rushed
21. show how
22. task
23. uncertain
24. unclear
25. unfamiliar

58   See Conversation Springboards on page 106.

Picture Discussion

With your class, answer the questions about the picture story. • Use the vocabulary list. • Add more words.

1. What is happening in each scene?
2. What is good about this woman's first day on the job? What is bad?
3. How do her co-workers treat her? Why?
4. Why does she have each problem?
5. How does she feel at the end of the day? Why?

What's the Story?

Partner's Name _____

With a partner, create a story for this new employee. • Tell the story to another pair of students. • Be sure to answer these questions.

1. What is her name?
2. What is her job?
3. What work experience has she had?
4. Will she succeed at this job? Why or why not?

Group Problem Solving

In groups of four, discuss possible solutions to the young woman's problems at work. • Decide what advice to give her for the next day at work. • Report your advice to the class.

Share Your Story

Tell the class about a good or bad experience at a new job.

59

INSTRUCTIONS AT WORK

1. assume
2. check
3. clarification
4. clarify
5. confused
6. confusion
7. demonstrate
8. demonstration
9. double-check
10. expect
11. expectation
12. figure out
13. follow
14. illustrate
15. illustration
16. instruction manual
17. misunderstand
18. mix up
19. mix-up
20. overlook
21. perplexed
22. puzzled
23. repeat
24. request
25. sequence
26. skip a step
27. specific
28. specifically
29. take for granted

Picture Discussion

With your class, answer the questions about the scenes. • Use the vocabulary list. • Add more words.

1. What is happening in each scene?
2. What went wrong in these situations? Why?
3. What will happen next in each scene?
4. How is it possible to avoid these problems?

See Conversation Springboards on pages 106 and 107.

What Do You Say? What Do You Do?

In groups of three, decide what to say and do in each of these situations. • Share your solutions with another group. • Role-play one solution for the class.

- ◆ You don't know how to switch a phone call to another employee's extension. You have no instructions.
- ◆ You are typing a report which is due at the end of the day. Your computer just "crashed." You don't have the instruction manual.
- ◆ You work at the counter in a cafeteria and can't understand a customer.
- ◆ You deliver packages to a house where a very large dog chases you every time you approach.

Community Activity

Find a set of instructions at home, at work, or in an office or agency in your community (how to operate a washing machine, how to use a copy machine, how to use an ATM card). • Bring the instructions to class. • Read them with your classmates and figure them out together. • Are the instructions clear?

Write with a Partner   Partner's Name _____

With a partner, choose one of the following tasks. • Write a set of instructions for the task. • Read your instructions to another pair, and have them pantomime the task. (Make sure you include every step of the task!)

- ◆ wash clothes in a washing machine
- ◆ connect a VCR to a TV
- ◆ operate a standard shift car
- ◆ hang a picture on a wall
- ◆ plant a tree
- ◆ other: _____

Speech

Demonstrate a procedure for your class. • Choose a procedure that you know well (preparing a special dish, explaining a math problem, performing a special dance step, using a special piece of equipment). • Bring to class everything you need to make your demonstration clear. • Use the board for written instructions.

DOING A GOOD JOB

1. alert	8. courteous	15. initiative
2. bad attitude	9. crush	16. interested
3. bag groceries	10. diligent	17. pride
4. careful	11. discourteous	18. reach
5. careless	12. good attitude	19. stack
6. clock in	13. hardworking	20. teamwork
7. conscientious	14. industrious	21. work habits

Picture Discussion

With your class, answer the questions about the scenes. • Use the vocabulary list. • Add more words.

1. What is happening in each scene?
2. In what ways are these workers doing a good job?
3. Which workers need to improve their work habits? Why?
4. What other ways are there to doing a good job in a supermarket? in a factory? in a fast food restaurant? in a bank? in an office? Make a list on the board.

62   See Conversation Springboards on page 108.

Group Problem Solving

In groups of three, discuss this problem and agree on a solution. • Report your solution to the class.

◆ You are one of the workers in these scenes who is doing a good job. Your co-worker is *not* doing a good job. What can you do to improve the situation?

Group Role Play

In the same groups, create these two role plays. • Present your role plays to the class.

◆ The manager is talking to a worker who is doing a good job.
◆ The manager is talking to a worker who is doing a bad job.

Partner Activity: Ask Aunt Betty

Partner's Name _____

With a partner, read and discuss this letter. • Together, write a response from Aunt Betty, *giving advice to* Frustrated in Fresno. *• Read your letter to the class.*

Ask Aunt Betty

Dear Aunt Betty:
    I work in an office with four co-workers. Three of us arrive on time every day, work hard, and often stay late to finish our work. One person, however, is often late, takes long breaks, and doesn't work very hard. The three of us usually have to finish <u>his</u> work! What should we do?

Frustrated in Fresno

INJURIES AT WORK

1. beaker
2. blow up
3. burst
4. chemical experiment
5. combustible
6. combustion
7. conveyor belt
8. explode
9. explosion
10. flammable
11. flask
12. fumes
13. ignite
14. inflammable
15. laboratory
16. protective gear
17. recoil
18. shatter
19. shoot/fire
20. throw one's back out
21. warning sign

Picture Discussion

With your class, answer the questions about the scenes. • Use the vocabulary list. • Add more words.

1. What is happening in each scene?
2. What injuries will each worker have?
3. What kinds of protective clothing or gear should some of these workers be wearing? What other kinds of protective clothing do people wear at work? Make a list on the board.
4. What kinds of warning signs are in the scenes? What other warning signs do you see at work? Make a list on the board.
5. Will workers' compensation pay for the medical care of these workers? Why or why not?
6. Which jobs are more dangerous than others?

64　　　　　　　　　　　See Conversation Springboards on page 108.

Group Problem Solving

In groups of three, discuss ways to prevent the problem in each scene. • Decide on the best prevention. • Report your preventive solutions to the class.

Group Brainstorm

In the same groups, choose a recorder. • List hazards at your jobs and in your homes. • Read your list to the class. • Make a class list on the board.

Share Your Story

In the same groups, answer these questions and share your stories. • Tell your best stories to the class.

1. Did you ever get hurt at work? What happened?
2. Did you ever get hurt doing work at home? What happened?

Community Activities

In groups of four, visit a work site in your community.

◆ Look for safety signs.
◆ Ask about safety regulations.
◆ Report your observations to the class.

Find safety regulations at your job. • Bring a copy of the regulations to class, and tell the class about them.

Draw with a Partner   Partner's Name _____

With a partner, discuss any safety signs you have seen around your community. • Draw the signs. • Explain them to another pair of students.

DEDUCTIONS FROM PAY

1. city withholding tax
2. credit union
3. direct deposit
4. earn
5. employee contribution
6. Federal Insurance Contributions Act (FICA)
7. federal withholding tax
8. gross earnings
9. gross pay
10. insurance deduction
11. labor union
12. Medicare tax
13. net earnings
14. payday
15. pay period
16. paystub
17. retirement contribution
18. salary after taxes
19. Social Security (FICA)
20. statement of earnings and deductions
21. state withholding tax
22. take-home pay
23. union dues

Picture Discussion

With your class, answer the questions about the scene. • Use the vocabulary list. • Add more words.

1. What is happening in this scene?
2. Why is the one employee unhappy?
3. What deductions show on her paycheck?
4. What is her co-worker telling her?
5. Do you understand each of these payroll deductions?
6. Why does her co-worker's paycheck look different?

See Conversation Springboards on page 108.

Partner Role Play

Partner's Name _____

With a partner, create a role play between an employee and a payroll office clerk. • Present your role play to another pair of students.

The employee wants to do three things:

1. change his or her paycheck to direct deposit.
2. open an account in the employee credit union and have $5 deducted every week.
3. report an error—he or she worked 3 hours overtime last week, but didn't get paid for the overtime.

Cross-Cultural Exchange

In groups of four, choose a conversation monitor and a recorder. • Discuss these questions. • Compare cultures when possible. • Report the results of your discussion to the class.

1. Are taxes withheld from paychecks in your country?
2. What other deductions from paychecks are there?
3. Are paychecks deposited directly into banks?
4. What workers belong to unions? Are unions powerful?

Class Survey

With your class, ask these questions. • Compare your responses with your classmates.

1. Did you ever have Medicare tax or Social Security contributions deducted from your income?
2. Do you know anyone who receives Social Security checks?
3. Do you think Social Security is a good government program?
4. Do you think income tax withholding is a good government program?
5. Did you ever belong to a labor union?
6. Did you ever have paychecks direct-deposited?

Group Brainstorm

In groups of three, choose a recorder. • List things that can be deducted from paychecks. • Compare and combine your list with another group. • Read your combined list to the class. • Make a class list on the board.

SPENDING MONEY

1. bad credit
2. budget
3. common sense
4. credit rating
5. credit risk
6. debt
7. disposable income
8. economize
9. entertainment expenses
10. expenditure
11. expenses
12. extravagance
13. extravagant
14. financial responsibility
15. good credit
16. good sense
17. impress
18. live above one's means
19. live within one's means
20. moderation
21. overspend
22. owe
23. prudent
24. repossess
25. sensible
26. simple pleasures
27. spendthrift
28. splurge
29. waste
30. wasteful

Picture Discussion

With your class, answer the questions about the picture story. • Use the vocabulary list. • Add more words.

1. How do these co-workers spend their paychecks?
2. What other differences do you think there are in their lives?
3. What do you think their beliefs are about spending money?
4. Tell each story.

See Conversation Springboards on page 108.

Group Brainstorm

In groups of three, choose a recorder. • List ways to save money in everyday expenses. • Read your list to the class. • Make a class list on the board. • Which advice is the most useful?

Conversation Squares

In the same groups, fill in the chart. • First write your own answers. • Then ask your partners the questions and write their answers. • Compare answers with another group.

	You	Partner 1	Partner 2
Student's Name			
What do you waste money on?			
Are you saving for anything? What?			
When you have extra money, what do you do with it?			

Group Problem Posing/Problem Solving

In the same groups, discuss ways people get into trouble spending money. • State each problem. • What advice would you give? • Report your problems and solutions to the class.

Class Game: Guess Who!

On a slip of paper, write one item you would like to splurge on. • Make a pile. • Pick a paper. • Read it to the class. • Guess who wrote it!

PAYING TAXES

1. accountant
2. annual income
3. auditor
4. back taxes
5. computation
6. compute
7. deadline
8. deductible
9. dependent
10. exempt
11. exemption
12. file a tax return
13. Form 1040
14. Form 1040EZ
15. Form W-2
16. income tax
17. Internal Revenue Service (IRS)
18. late penalty
19. nonresident
20. overpay
21. pay interest
22. resident
23. taxable income
24. tax credit
25. tax evasion
26. tax form(s)
27. taxpayer
28. tax withheld

Picture Discussion

With your class, answer the questions about the scenes. • Use the vocabulary list. • Add more words.

1. What is happening in each scene?
2. What is the happy woman looking at?
3. Why is one woman employee worried?
4. What is her co-worker explaining to her?
5. How many dependents does the co-worker have?
6. Who is L. Ross? What is she discussing with the man?
7. What did the unhappy man receive? Why is he so upset? What advice is he getting?

70   See Conversation Springboards on pages 108 and 109.

Partner Activity: *Ask Aunt Betty*

Partner's Name _____

With a partner, read and discuss this letter. • Together, write a reply from *Aunt Betty*, giving advice to *Worried in Washington*. • Read your letter to the class.

Ask Aunt Betty

Dear Aunt Betty:

My husband has a small business repairing lawn mowers and doing odd jobs, and I baby-sit for my neighbor's children. We make just enough money to pay for the rent and food. We can't even afford to take our kids to the dentist. But that's not the problem. I'm writing to you because we haven't filed an income tax return for three years. My husband says, "Forget it!" But I'm worried. What should I do?

Worried in Washington

Group Brainstorm

In groups of four, choose a recorder. • List things that the government spends tax money on. • Compare and combine your list with another group. • Read your combined list to the class. • Make a class list on the board.

Cross-Cultural Exchange

In the same groups, choose a conversation monitor and a recorder. • Discuss these questions. • Compare cultures when possible. • Report the results of your discussion to the class.

1. Compare taxes in different countries.
2. Is there a national income tax in your home country?
3. Who has to pay income tax?
4. What percentage of annual income do people have to pay?
5. When is the income tax due?
6. Is income tax withheld from people's wages?
7. What other kinds of taxes are there?

LEAVING A JOB

1 **2** **3**

1. advance
2. advancement
3. career change
4. career decision
5. career opportunity
6. career path
7. career training
8. give notice
9. leer
10. low pay
11. maternity leave
12. move away
13. overworked
14. regret
15. resign
16. resignation
17. seasonal layoff
18. self-improvement
19. sexual advance
20. stare
21. stressful
22. technical training
23. underpaid
24. working conditions

Picture Discussion

With your class, answer the questions about the picture story. • Use the vocabulary list. • Add more words.

1. What is happening in each scene?
2. What was this woman's reason for leaving each job?
3. What career opportunities did she have?
4. When did she retire? How old was she?
5. Tell the story of this woman's working life.

72   See Conversation Springboards on page 109.

Partner Role Play   Partner's Name _____

With a partner, choose one of the scenes. • Create a role play between the woman and her employer. • Include the reason for leaving, the employer's response, and the final goodbye. • Present your role play to the class.

Partner Interview   Partner's Name _____

Ask a partner these questions. • Then report your partner's responses to another pair of students.

1. Have you ever left a job? Why or why not?
2. Would you keep a bad job if you really needed the money? Why or why not?
3. What makes a job good?
4. What makes a job bad?

Group Brainstorm

In groups of four, choose a recorder. • List reasons for leaving a job. • Read your list to the class. • Make a class list on the board.

Group Decision

In the same groups, decide whether to keep each of these jobs or leave it. • Explain your decisions to the class.

- You have worked at this job for three years, but you have never had a raise. You are a good worker, but your employer cannot afford to pay you more.
- Your boss always tells the workers that they are lazy, slow, and incompetent. In fact, you and your co-workers are responsible, efficient, and careful.
- One of your co-workers has been making sexual advances towards you. You have tried to discourage this, but the situation continues to get worse.

REVIEW

Group Brainstorm

In groups of three, choose a recorder. • List the differences between doing a good job and doing a bad job. • Read your list to the class. • Make a class list on the board.

DIFFERENCES

Doing a Good Job	Doing a Bad Job
_____	_____
_____	_____
_____	_____
_____	_____
_____	_____

Partner Questions   Partner's Name _____

With a partner, make a list of questions to ask when starting a new job. • Include questions about job benefit details, payroll deductions, and income taxes. • Ask another pair your questions, and answer theirs. • Report your questions and answers to the class.

Partner Activity: Ask Aunt Betty

Partner's Name _____

With a partner, write a letter from Aunt Betty, giving advice to someone starting a new job. • Read your letter to the class.

Partner Game: What Do You Remember?

Partner's Name _____

With a partner, list as many employment problems from this unit as you can remember. • Check your list with another pair. • Look back through the unit. • Did you forget any of the problems?

Group Discussion

In groups of three, choose a recorder. • List reasons for leaving a job and reasons for staying at a job. • Compare your reasons with another group. • Discuss these questions.

1. When is it good to leave a job?
2. When is it better to stay?

UNIT 5
IN THE NEWS

76 Class News
78 News Media
80 Weather and Natural Disasters
82 Sports News
84 Entertainment News
86 Crime in the News
88 Heroes in the News
90 Local News
92 World News
94 Politics and Government in the News
96 Review

LEARNING STRATEGIES

- Every day that you are studying this unit, bring in a related article from a newspaper or magazine and tell the class about it.

- Watch a newscast every day in English. Note the channel, time, and newscasters. Note the news of the day. Make a list of the different topics covered. Then write down questions about the newscast. What was confusing? What didn't you understand?

- Watch sports news on TV or read the sports section of a local newspaper. Then answer these questions:
  - What sports are in the national news now? Why?
  - What athletes are in the news now? Why?
  - What is the biggest current sports story?
  - What local sports are in the news now?

CLASS NEWS

1. catch up
2. champion
3. championship
4. ecstatic
5. elated
6. embrace
7. homecoming
8. hug
9. MVP (Most Valuable Player)
10. overjoyed
11. overwhelmed
12. personal news
13. reunion
14. reunite
15. separation
16. shock
17. slip and fall
18. special occasion
19. teammate
20. tears of joy
21. thrill
22. thrilled
23. thrilling
24. triumph
25. trophy
26. unforgettable moment
27. victorious
28. victory

See Conversation Springboards on page 109.

Picture Discussion

With your class, answer the questions about the scenes. • Use the vocabulary list. • Add more words.

1. Why is the woman's arm in a sling? Tell the story of her accident.
2. Why are the young man's teammates carrying him? Tell the story of their victory.
3. Why does the young woman look so surprised? Tell the story of her happiness.
4. Why is the man hugging his twin brother? Tell the story of their reunion.

Draw with a Partner   Partner's Name _____

Decide what news you have to share. • Draw a picture of your news. • Explain your picture to a partner. • Show your pictures to another pair. • Explain your partner's picture.

Group Superlatives

In groups of four, answer these questions. • Report your answers to the class.

1. Who has had the best week?
2. Who has had the worst week?
3. Who has had the best news this year?
4. Who has the most exciting plans for this weekend?
5. Who has the most unusual news story to tell?

Write with the Class

With your class, write a newsletter or make a bulletin board for class news. • Bring pictures and make a headline for each news story.

Community Activity

Call a friend or relative to catch up on the latest news. • Take notes on your friend's or relative's news. • In groups of four, report on your telephone conversation.

NEWS MEDIA

1. anchorperson
2. article
3. at the scene
4. bulletin
5. cable network news
6. current event
7. front page
8. headline
9. live broadcast
10. newscast
11. newscaster
12. newsmagazine
13. newsperson
14. on location
15. on-line news
16. reporter
17. report the news
18. satellite news
19. station
20. telecast
21. top story
22. weekly

Picture Discussion

With your class, answer the questions about the scenes. • Use the vocabulary list. • Add more words.

1. In what different ways does this family get the news?
2. What time do you think it is? Why?
3. What TV program are they watching? Why?
4. What is the top story on the TV news?
5. What is the headline on the front page of the newspaper?
6. What kind of magazine is the mother reading?
7. What news is the student looking at on his computer?

See Conversation Springboards on page 110.

Find Someone Who

Review the vocabulary with your teacher. • Add to this list. • Then interview your classmates and fill in the name of someone who . . .

1. reads a daily newspaper. _____

2. reads a weekly newsmagazine. _____

3. listens to the news on the radio. _____

4. watches cable network news. _____

5. watched the news on TV yesterday. _____

6. _____ _____

7. _____ _____

Class Discussion

With your class, make a list on the board of people in the news. • How many names does everyone recognize? • Why are these people in the news?

Group Role Play

In groups of four, create a role play between a person in the news and news reporters. • Plan questions for the reporters to ask, and prepare answers to the questions. • Present your role play to the class.

Community Activity

Watch the news on TV in English and take notes. • Report back to the class. • Include answers to these questions.

1. What stories were in the news?
2. Where did they occur?
3. What happened?
4. How much did you understand?

WEATHER AND NATURAL DISASTERS

1. avalanche	12. earthquake	23. powerful	_____
2. blizzard	13. erupt	24. rescuer	_____
3. burn down	14. eruption	25. rubble	_____
4. catastrophe	15. escape	26. shake	_____
5. collapse	16. evacuate	27. survival	_____
6. deadly	17. evacuation	28. terrify	_____
7. destroy	18. forecast	29. thunderous	_____
8. destruction	19. forest fire	30. tidal wave	_____
9. devastating	20. hurricane	31. tornado	_____
10. drought	21. lava	32. towering	_____
11. dry up	22. level	33. volcano	_____

Picture Discussion

With your class, answer the questions about the scenes. • Use the vocabulary list. • Add more words.

1. What natural disaster is shown on each TV screen?
2. What is happening in each catastrophe?
3. What other natural disasters are there? Describe them, and add them to the list.
4. Where can these catastrophes occur?
5. Which natural disasters can be forecast? Which cannot?

See Conversation Springboards on page 110.

Cross-Cultural Exchange

In groups of four, choose a conversation monitor and a recorder. • Discuss these questions. • Compare cultures when possible. • Report the results of your discussion to the class.

1. What kind of natural disasters occur in your country?
2. How often do they occur? Are they seasonal? When was the last one? How many people were affected?
3. How do people prepare for the disaster? What precautions are taken in extreme conditions? What do they do afterward?
4. Who has experienced a natural disaster? Ask questions about the experience.

Group Vocabulary Challenge

*In the same groups, list different kinds of weather. • Work fast! • Read your list to the class. • Which group has the longest list? • Make a class list on the board. • Copy the new words in the **Vocabulary** section of your notebook.*

Community Activity

Watch a weather report on TV, and read a weather forecast in a newspaper. • Answer these questions.

1. What is today's high temperature?
2. What was last night's low temperature?
3. What is the forecast for tomorrow?
4. What is the extended forecast for the week?
5. Are there any extreme weather conditions being forecast? Where? What are they?

Cross-Cultural Role Play

Pretend you are a TV weather reporter in your hometown. • Create a role play, reporting the weather for a typical day there. • Present your role play to the class.

- Include the high and low temperatures and an extended forecast.
- Use visual aids.
- Refer to a map.

SPORTS NEWS

PH BIG WORLD OF SPORTS

1. amateur athlete
2. athlete
3. athletic
4. balance beam
5. bronze medal
6. commentator
7. compete
8. competition
9. competitive
10. figure skating
11. finalist
12. gold medal
13. indoor sport
14. international competition
15. medalist
16. mixed pairs
17. Olympics
18. outdoor sport
19. pole vault
20. professional athlete
21. semi-finalist
22. silver medal
23. skating rink
24. sports event
25. stadium
26. track and field

See Conversation Springboards on pages 110 and 111.

Picture Discussion

With your class, answer the questions about the scenes. • Use the vocabulary list. • Add more words.

1. What sports event is on each TV screen?
2. What international competition could this be?
3. Are these athletes amateurs or professionals? Explain your answer.
4. Which sports are indoor sports? Which are outdoor sports? Where do people play each sport?
5. What other track and field events are there? Make a list on the board.
6. In what other sports events do athletes compete internationally? Make a list on the board.

Group Vocabulary Challenge

*In groups of three, choose one sport that you know well. • List vocabulary for that sport. • Work fast! • Read your list to the class. • Which group has the longest list? • Make a class list on the board. • Copy the new words in the **Vocabulary** section of your notebook.*

Speech

Tell the class about a sport you have played, or a sport that you like very much. • Bring related equipment to class, if possible. • Explain the sport. • Show the class how to play it.

Group Discussion

In groups of three, choose a recorder. • Discuss these questions. • Share your information with another group.

1. What sports injuries are common?
2. How do they happen?
3. How can they be prevented?
4. Are any sports too dangerous or too violent?

Cross-Cultural Exchange

In the same groups, choose a conversation monitor and a recorder. • Discuss these questions. • Compare cultures when possible. • Report the results of your discussion to the class.

1. What sports are most popular in your country?
2. Which sports season is it in your country now?
3. Who are the most famous athletes in your country?

ENTERTAINMENT NEWS

1. acrobat
2. celebrity
3. classical music
4. clown
5. conduct
6. conductor
7. entertain
8. entertainer
9. entertaining
10. family entertainment
11. limited engagement
12. magic
13. magical
14. magician
15. performer
16. stage
17. star
18. symphony orchestra
19. theme park
20. tightrope walker
21. trapeze artist

See Conversation Springboards on page 111.

Picture Discussion

With your class, answer the questions about the scenes. • Use the vocabulary list. • Add more words.

1. What kind of entertainment does each scene show?
2. What is happening in each scene?
3. What kind of entertainment will this family choose? Why?
4. What other kinds of entertainment would the daughter enjoy? Draw one example in the empty bubble.
5. What other kinds of entertainment are there?
6. What kinds of entertainment are most popular? Why?
7. What kinds of entertainment are in the news now? Why?
8. What entertainment celebrities are in the news? Why?

Who Else?

List three of your favorite forms of entertainment. • Then find classmates who have the same favorites. • Write their names in the chart and report your findings to the class.

	Favorite Form of Entertainment	Student's Name
1.		1. _____ 2. _____ 3. _____
2.		1. _____ 2. _____ 3. _____
3.		1. _____ 2. _____ 3. _____

Group Role Play

In groups of three, create a role play of a TV or radio talk show host interviewing two celebrities. • Present your role play to the class. • Have the class participate by asking questions.

Community Activity

*Bring a newspaper to class. • In groups of four, look for any local entertainment. • Is there an event that everyone would like to attend? • Make arrangements with the class, and attend the event together. • Then write a **Journal** entry and discuss the event in class afterwards. • Answer these questions.*

◆ Did you enjoy the event?
◆ What did you like about it?
◆ What didn't you like?

CRIME IN THE NEWS

1. acquit	14. defend	27. murder
2. acquittal	15. defendant	28. prosecute
3. assault	16. defense	29. prosecution
4. attorney	17. guilty	30. punish
5. bailiff	18. handgun	31. punishment
6. capital punishment	19. innocent	32. rob
7. cell	20. jail	33. robbery
8. commit	21. juror	34. sentence
9. convict	22. jury	35. testify
10. conviction	23. justice	36. testimony
11. courtroom	24. lawyer	37. trial
12. criminal	25. mug	38. verdict
13. deadly weapon	26. mugging	39. witness stand

See Conversation Springboards on page 111.

Picture Discussion

With your class, answer the questions about the picture story. • Use the vocabulary list. • Add more words.

1. What crime, or crimes, did the man commit?
2. Who is the witness at the trial? What is her testimony?
3. What will the jury's verdict be?
4. What sentence will the judge give?
5. Tell the whole story of this crime in the news.
6. What would you do if you were the victim in this crime? the witness? the attorneys? the jury?
7. What other kinds of crime are there?

Cross-Cultural Exchange

In groups of four, choose a conversation monitor and a recorder. • Discuss these questions. • Compare cultures when possible. • Report the results of your discussion to the class.

1. What kinds of crime are most common in your country?
2. What kinds of punishment are there?
3. Are there different punishments for children and for adults?
4. Is capital punishment used in your country?

School Survey

Ask three people in your school this question. • Fill in their answers. • Report your findings to the class. • What are the total class results?

Do You Approve of Capital Punishment?

1. Yes ☐   No ☐   Not Sure ☐
2. Yes ☐   No ☐   Not Sure ☐
3. Yes ☐   No ☐   Not Sure ☐

Community Activity

Bring in local newspapers. • Discuss articles about crimes in the newspapers with your class. • Watch local TV news. • List crimes reported on TV. • Bring your list to class. • Compare the list with the newspaper articles and discuss with your class.

HEROES IN THE NEWS

1. admiration	10. heroic	19. patriotic	
2. admire	11. heroism	20. patriotism	
3. brave	12. honor	21. protect	
4. bravery	13. leader	22. risk	
5. cause	14. martyr	23. sacrifice	
6. courage	15. medal	24. saint	
7. courageous	16. memorial	25. statue	
8. dedicated	17. monument	26. strength	
9. die for	18. patriot	27. veteran	

See Conversation Springboards on page 112.

Picture Discussion

With your class, answer the questions about the scenes. • Use the vocabulary list. • Add more words.

1. Where are the boy and his mother visiting? What statue is the boy looking at? What do you think his mother will tell him?
2. What heroes are pictured on coins and bills in the currency of your country?
3. What heroic actions did these people perform?
4. In what ways do we honor heroes? List them on the board.

Draw with a Partner   Partner's Name _____

With a partner, choose a hero you admire. • Draw a picture of the hero and write a caption for your picture. • Explain your picture and caption to another pair. • Report your choices to the class.

Conversation Squares

In groups of three, fill in the chart. • First write your own answers. • Then ask your partners the questions and write their answers. • Compare answers with another group.

	You	**Partner 1**	**Partner 2**
Student's Name			
Who is your personal hero?			
Why?			

Group Decision

In the same groups, decide who should win the "Local Hero Award" this year. • Report your decision to the class and explain your choice.

- A fireman who rescued a family from a fire. The fireman was badly burned during the rescue.
- A twelve-year-old girl who has AIDS. She is very brave and has made many speeches to help raise money for AIDS research.
- A fifteen-year-old boy who rescued an elderly woman from an attacker. The boy was shot in the arm during the rescue.
- A woman astronaut who was chosen to be the captain of a space shuttle mission.

Cross-Cultural Exchange

In the same groups, choose a conversation monitor and a recorder. • Discuss these questions. • Compare cultures when possible. • Report the results of your discussion to the class. • Make a class list on the board.

1. What international heroes, martyrs, and saints does everyone in the class know about?
2. How are heroes honored in your country? Give some examples.
3. What martyrs are admired in your culture? What did they do?

LOCAL NEWS

1. car crash
2. cleanup
3. dumpsite
4. fall apart
5. head-on collision
6. health hazard
7. human interest story
8. illegal dumping
9. kidnap
10. local issue
11. missing
12. multi-vehicle accident
13. overcrowded
14. pileup
15. pollutant
16. pollute
17. polluter
18. toxic waste
19. unsafe conditions

See Conversation Springboards on page 112.

Picture Discussion

With your class, answer the questions about the scenes. • Use the vocabulary list. • Add more words.

1. What is happening in each TV news scene?
2. What do you think caused the car accident?
3. What is the condition of the school? What improvements are needed?
4. What do you think was dumped illegally?
5. What do you think happened to the child?
6. What local issues are in this TV newscast?

Group Role Play

In groups of three, choose one of the stories in this TV newscast. • Create a role play of a news reporter interviewing people at the scene of the story. • Ask questions about the story. • Explain what happened. • Present your role play to the class.

Community Activity

Bring a local newspaper to class. • In the same groups, find headlines and page numbers of the items below. • Report your findings to the class. • Discuss the most interesting local news together.

◆ local events coming soon
◆ local problems and issues in the news
◆ local good news

Class Brainstorm

With your class, choose a recorder. • List on the board the local problems and issues. • How many items are on the list? • Now list the local good news. • How many items are on this list?

Group Problem Posing/Problem Solving

In groups of four, choose one local problem or issue in the news. • Define the problem or issue. • Decide on a solution. • Report your solution to the class.

Cross-Cultural Exchange

In the same groups, choose a conversation monitor and a recorder. • Discuss these questions. • Compare cultures when possible. • Report the results of your discussion to the class.

1. What local problems and issues are most common in your hometown?
2. What is the current local news in your hometown? Tell it to your group.

WORLD NEWS

1. aid
2. armed
3. battle
4. breakthrough
5. famine
6. fighting
7. hijack
8. hostage
9. humanitarian
10. international incident
11. military
12. oil spill
13. Red Cross
14. refugee
15. research scientist
16. scientific discovery
17. starvation
18. starve
19. supplies
20. tank
21. terrorism
22. terrorist
23. Third World
24. underdeveloped
25. war
26. wipe out

92   See Conversation Springboards on pages 112 and 113.

Picture Discussion

With your class, answer the questions about the scenes. • Use the vocabulary list. • Add more words.

1. What is happening in each TV news scene?
2. Where in the world is there a war or fighting right now?
3. Where in the world has there been a famine recently? terrorism?
4. What scientific discoveries have been reported in the news recently?
5. What effect will the oil spill have on the environment? Explain.
6. What good news has been in the world news recently?

Group Decision

In groups of four, decide what the story is for each TV news scene and where each story is happening. • Write one headline for each story, and report your headlines to another group.

Group Problem Posing

In the same groups, list some current world problems. • Report your list to the class. • Make a class list on the board. • With your group, decide on the three most serious problems in the world today. • Report your problems to the class. • Which problems does the whole class think are the most serious?

Class Brainstorm

With your class, choose a recorder. • List on the board ideas for solving the three most serious world problems. • Which are the best ideas?

Community Activity

Watch the world news on TV, and take notes on these questions. • Report your notes to the class.

- What countries are in the world news?
- What problems are in the world news?
- What good news did you see?

Cross-Cultural Exchange

In groups of four, choose a conversation monitor and a recorder. • Discuss these questions. • Compare cultures when possible. • Report the results of your discussion to the class.

1. What is the most serious problem or issue in your country right now?
2. What people are in the news in your country right now? Why are they in the news?
3. What good things are happening in your country right now?

POLITICS AND GOVERNMENT IN THE NEWS

1. assassinate	11. dictator	21. political party
2. assassination	12. dictatorship	22. politician
3. ballot	13. elect	23. protest
4. ballot box	14. election	24. protestor
5. bodyguard	15. legislature	25. rally
6. campaign	16. march	26. representative
7. candidate	17. military coup	27. riot
8. debate	18. official	28. speaker
9. democracy	19. overthrow	29. supporter
10. democratic	20. picket	30. vote

Picture Discussion

With your class, answer the questions about the scenes. • Use the vocabulary list. • Add more words.

1. What political events do these news scenes show? What is happening in each scene?
2. In what countries could each of these events be happening?
3. How many kinds of government can you think of? List them on the board.

See Conversation Springboards on page 113.

Cross-Cultural Exchange

In groups of four, choose a conversation monitor and a recorder. • Discuss these questions. • Compare cultures when possible. • Report the results of your discussion to the class.

1. What kind of government exists in your country? Describe it.
2. Who is the head of the government? What is the leader's title?
3. Do people trust election results in your country? Why or why not?
4. What political parties are in your country? Who supports each party?

Find Someone Who

Review the vocabulary with your teacher. • Add to this list. • Then interview your classmates and fill in the name of someone who . . .

1. doesn't like politics. _____
2. is a member of a political party. _____
3. has voted in an election. _____
4. has participated in a protest. _____
5. has voted by absentee ballot. _____
6. _____ _____
7. _____ _____

Dialog Journal

*Write a **Journal** entry about one of your political views. • Then read your entry to a partner. • Ask questions about your partner's entry.*

Guest Speaker

Write a class letter inviting a local politician or elected official to speak to your class. • Prepare questions for the speaker. • Take notes during the speech. • Write a class thank-you letter after the speech.

REVIEW

Group Vocabulary Challenge

In groups of four, make two lists: Good News and Bad News. • Add the appropriate news stories to the lists. • Which list is longer? • Why? • Compare your lists with another group.

Partner Role Play   Partner's Name _____

With a partner, choose a celebrity to interview on a TV newscast. • Write ten questions for the interview. • Create a role play of the interview. • Present the role play to the class.

Conversation Squares

In groups of three, fill in the chart. • First write your own answers. • Then ask your partners the questions and write their answers. • Compare answers with another group.

	You	Partner 1	Partner 2
Student's Name			
Who are your personal heroes?			
What do you think is the worst crime?			
What do you think is the best world news recently?			
What do you think is the worst world news recently?			
Who are your favorite entertainers? What do they do?			

Class Role Play

With your class, plan a complete TV newscast. • Divide into groups to cover each aspect of the news. • Include these news segments. • Present them to your teacher!

- ◆ headline news
- ◆ world trouble spot satellite report
- ◆ on-the-scene crime report
- ◆ sports
- ◆ weather
- ◆ entertainment report

APPENDIX

Conversation Springboards	98
Grammar for Conversation Contents	114
Grammar for Conversation	115
Maps	
Africa	125
Asia and Australia	126
Europe	127
North, Central, and South America	128
United States of America (U.S.A.) and Canada	129
Speech/Audience Evaluation Forms	130
Activities Guide	131
Alphabetical Word List to Picture Dictionary	142

CONVERSATION SPRINGBOARDS

UNIT 1: HOUSING

PLACES TO LIVE (pp. 2–3)

Conversation Springboard: *What's happening?*

M1: We just sold our house!
F1: Wow, that was fast!
M1: Yeah, the people who bought from us live in a high-rise in the city. They think our little ranch house is big!
F2: Yeah, the house sold quite easily. The real estate market is strong because the area is really growing.
M1: Yes, there are housing developments being built everywhere—it's no longer the village it once was. That's why Anne and I are moving out—this town is getting too congested. There's just no space anymore.
F1: Where do you think you'll live?
M1: Oh, I don't know. Maybe a log cabin, somewhere in the countryside.
F2: Excuse me, Tom? A log cabin in the countryside? I think I'd rather move back to the city—to a town house.
M1: A town house, Anne? I didn't think you wanted to move *back* to the city—and to live in a *town house!*

Picture Conversation: *Finish the conversation.*

M1: It's been so discouraging looking for a place to live!
F1: We've seen some pretty nice places, but they're all so different!
M1: Well, which do you prefer, Maria? We have to make a decision soon!

F1: _____
M1: _____
F1: _____

INSIDE YOUR HOME (pp. 4-5)

Conversation Springboard: *What's next?*

M1: Sylvia, I sure am glad we found this town house! It's perfect for us! Let's try to finish putting up the wallpaper and mini-blinds tonight before we go to bed.
F1: I never hung wallpaper before. It's a good thing we didn't put the carpets down yet—we're making such a mess!
M1: You said it! And it's a good thing the furniture doesn't arrive until next week.
F1: That's for sure. You know, this room is going to look really nice after all the furnishings are in place.
M1: It sure will. The last occupant's taste was pretty awful—I mean, I couldn't live with black walls and ceilings—it would feel like a cave!
F1: I know. Lighter colors make a room look so much more spacious.
M1: By the way, how do you want to redecorate the bedroom?

Picture Springboard: *Finish the conversation.*

F1: I really like our new neighbors.
M1: Yeah? I haven't met them yet.
F1: They're very nice. You should see their apartment. It's decorated beautifully.
M1: Really? What's it like?

F1: _____
M1: _____
F1: _____

FINDING THE RIGHT HOME (pp. 6-7)

Conversation Springboard: *What's your opinion?*

(TV commercial)

M1: Today's Homes Realtor offers a special group of homes in your area. We have a lovely one-family home on a large lot—a handyman's dream. Three bedrooms, two baths, and an above-ground pool—asking price is $55,000. A great bargain!
Or, if you prefer a mobile home, we have several available within your price range. Great condition, some with dishwashers and wall-to-wall carpeting. All in Shady Oaks Trailer Park.
Condos your style? How about a two-bedroom town house for $100,000. Low down payment and low interest loans available! Near transportation, shopping, and schools.
We have great rental properties, too! How about a studio for $400 a month. This apartment is in excellent condition. Believe it or not, a new refrigerator, dishwasher, heat, and utilities are included in this great bargain! Fenced-in yard and laundry room, too—what a deal!

Picture Springboard: *Finish the conversation.*

M1: We've been looking for weeks, Sheldon. I'm not sure that we'll ever find something that will fit our budget.
M2: Dad, don't worry—we will. Be patient. We know exactly what we need and the real estate agent is working hard to help us.
F1: Oh, look at this house! What do you think? Do you like it?

M2: _____
M1: _____
F1: _____

UTILITY PROBLEMS (pp. 8–9)

Conversation Springboard: *What happened?*

M1: What a storm last night!
M2: Don't remind me!
M1: Why? What happened?
M2: The power went out, and. . .

M1: You, too? The power was out in our neighborhood for over an hour.
M2: The funny thing is the power *did* go out—but the storm wasn't the cause.
M1: Oh?
M2: That's right. We were sitting in the dark for hours waiting for the power to come back on, when the entire time a fuse had just blown.
M1: You're kidding!
M2: No. I found out later that my kids had their computer, blow-dryer, TV, and CD player plugged into the same extension cord! It's no wonder the house didn't burn down!
M1: That *is* pretty dangerous.
M2: Yeah. You know, I never even thought to check the fuse box. I mean, I just figured it was the storm outside that knocked out the power. . . Hmm, I really should get an electrician to come in and rewire the place. . .

Picture Conversation: *Finish the conversation.*
M1: Good morning. Star Oil.
M2: Yes, this is Juan Ramirez. My oil tank just ran out of oil.
M1: Please hold. . .
M2: Wait! I'm calling from a pay phone—you see, my phone was. . .
M1: Could you please repeat that, sir?
M2: _____
M1: _____
M2: _____

TENANTS AND LANDLORDS (pp. 10-11)
Conversation Springboard: *What's next?*
M1: We really want to get out of our lease. We've got such terrible conditions in our apartment, we can't stand living there any more!
M2: Since when? I thought you loved that apartment, David.
M1: Well, since the new owner took over, the place has really deteriorated. Most of the major appliances don't work, and they refuse to fix them or replace them. They're not even functional! The fixtures in the bathroom are leaking. And they don't maintain the building.
M2: It's really the landlord's responsibility to keep everything serviceable.
F1: Rick's right—you don't need brand-new appliances, but it's fair to ask for decent, second-hand models if the ones you have can't be fixed.
M1: Oh, I've asked the landlord so many times. It doesn't do any good!
F2: You have rights to have the appliances be in working order. Why don't you call the tenant's rights organization? They can give you good advice.
M1: Great idea, Eliza. I'll do that today.

Picture Springboard: *Finish the conversation.*
F1: Mrs. Patel? This is Jean Samuels in Apartment 3C. The refrigerator really *does* need to be replaced. It's completely stopped working. All my food is spoiled, and the ice cream is melting all over the freezer.
F2: Are you sure? Check the temperature controls. Maybe the temperature needs to be adjusted.
F1: Mrs. Patel, it's not the temperature controls. We've been talking about replacing this refrigerator for a year now. I'm sorry, but I'm really annoyed about this.
F2: _____
F1: _____
F2: _____

INSURING YOUR PROPERTY (pp. 12-13)
Conversation Springboard: *What's happening?*
(telephone conversation)
M1: Hello, Mrs. Jones? Good evening. This is Sam Slick, Alpha Insurance representative in your neighborhood. How are you tonight?
F1: Excuse me. Alpha Insurance? I don't think you're my representative.
M1: Well, not right now. But I'm going to offer you a homeowner insurance protection plan against loss, burglary, storm, water, smoke and fire damage with the lowest premium on the market today.
F1: Excuse me. I don't understand. Could you speak more slowly, please?
M1: Sure. I'm about to offer you, tonight only, the best insurance plan you can get.
F1: Well, I don't really need an insurance plan.
M1: Mrs. Jones, everyone needs insurance. What if you are burglarized? What coverage would you have? What if a fire ruins everything you own?
F1: Mr. Slick, first of all I don't need any insurance. I live in a rented apartment, and all the furniture is rented, too. Secondly, my dinner's getting cold. So thanks, anyway. Bye.

Picture Springboard: *Finish the conversation.*
F1: Do you think our insurance will cover the fire and smoke damage?
M1: Let me get my clipboard and write up a report. As the insurance adjustor, all I can do is send in the report. I don't know about the extent of your coverage.
F1: I know my deductible is $250, but I sure hope the insurance covers the replacement cost.
M1: _____
F1: _____
M1: _____

MOVING (pp. 14-15)

Conversation Springboard: *What's happening?*

F1: They're gone just for a day, and I miss them already!
M1: Oh, Mom, Jeff got such a good job—it was too good to pass up. It was nice to help them pack, wasn't it?
F1: Well, I guess. With the children around, Lucy was having a hard time wrapping and packing all the glassware. She has so many fragile things.
M1: Well, you were great to help organize their belongings. There was so much confusion that so many of their things could have been broken or scratched. Hard to believe we did it ourselves without professional movers.
F1: Still, transporting everything in that utility trailer worries me. I hope we packed everything OK.
M1: Mom, don't worry. I'm sure everything's fine.
F1: Well, how will Lucy help Jeff with all those heavy boxes?
M1: Don't worry. They'll be fine... Oh, no!
F1: What? What's wrong?
M1: Look—Christopher forgot his teddy bear!

Picture Springboard: *Finish the conversation.*

M2: Christopher, don't cry. Tell Daddy what's wrong.
F2: Do you think he's sick?
M2: I can't imagine why he's so miserable.

F2: _____

M2: _____

ANSWERING THE DOOR (pp. 16-17)

Conversation Springboard: *What's the process?*

M1: We don't have much time for the Partner Activity.
F1: Let's try to finish before class is over.
M1: There's not much to do here.
F1: What do we have to do?
M1: Let's see, we need to read the letter and discuss it, and then write a reply.
F1: Hmm, I wonder if Aunt Betty is a real person. She looks real.
M1: And I wonder if her dog is real. The dog looks real, too. What do you think its name is?
F1: I don't know. A good name would be Sugar, though...
M1: Oops! We forgot to do the activity. Let's see. "With a partner, read and discuss this letter..."
Teacher: OK, class, that's it for today.

Picture Springboard: *Finish the conversation.*

(knocking at door)
F1: Who is it?
F2: It's Mary, Mrs. Smith. Mary Martinez.
F1: What do you want?

F2: _____
F1: _____
F2: _____

NEIGHBORHOOD PROBLEMS (pp. 18-19)

Conversation Springboard: *What's next?*

(TV reporter)
F1: This is Mary Wu reporting live from Williams Street. This neighborhood will be our first experiment in urban renewal. Let's see who we can talk to. Raf, you've lived here for 30 years. What can you tell our viewers?
M1: I've seen a lot of changes over the years. The neighborhood has really gotten run down. Lots of abandoned cars, boarded-up houses, gangs, and garbage on the streets.
F1: Thanks, Raf... Lilian Mendez, you have been an advocate for this neighborhood, trying to organize your neighbors now for a year. Have there been any improvements?
F2: Well, I'm sorry to say, very few. There's graffiti all over the place, vagrants hanging out on the street corners, and homeless people who have nothing to do. People are worried about their personal safety. It's sad, but I'm not ready to give up. We've got a petition going around to give to the mayor.
F1: Thanks, Lilian. Looks like you're doing a great job, but there's more work to be done! Back to you, Tom.

Picture Springboard: *Finish the conversation.*

M1: Lilian, you talked to the reporter. What did she say to you?
F2: Not much, Raf. But maybe with the publicity, we'll have a chance with our petition.
M1: I'm really tired of this dangerous neighborhood. I used to love it here. I felt safe and good about the community. Now, I'm almost ready to give up!

F2: _____
M1: _____
F2: _____

NEIGHBORHOOD IMPROVEMENTS (pp. 20-21)

Conversation Springboard: *What's happening?*

F2: Well, Raf, we did it! We really did it! Can you believe our neighborhood is going to be on the evening news as a good example of urban renewal?!
M1: *You* did it, Lilian. You never gave up. And look at it now.
F2: We *all* did it, Raf! One person can't change a neighborhood alone.
F1: Raf, Lilian, hi! The neighborhood looks wonderful! Your grass roots organization really succeeded. Mind if I interview a few people for the newscast?
F2: Go right ahead.
F1: Sir, what do you think of the changes in this neighborhood?
M2: I'm proud to be part of refurbishing the neighborhood. I used to be homeless, but the neighborhood association gave me a job. I'm leading the clean-up campaign, and everyone is helping. In all the years I've lived here, I haven't seen such warm, neighborly attitudes. It's wonderful!

F1: Thank you. Well, folks, you've seen it—this is amazing! Your tax dollars at their working best. And what it took were two really dedicated residents to start the ball rolling. This is Mary Wu, reporting live from Williams Street.

Picture Springboard: *Finish the conversation.*

M3: Look at this neighborhood. I moved away two years ago.
F1: And you don't recognize it, right?
M3: Yeah, so much has changed. I don't know where to begin!
F1: What do you think is the biggest change?
M3: _____
F1: _____
M3: _____

UNIT 2: TRANSPORTATION AND TRAVEL
COMMUTING (pp. 24-25)

Conversation Springboard: *What happened?*

M1: Hi, honey, you're home early.
F1: Boy, was I ever glad to be carpooling today!
M1: Really? I thought you said commuting with Andy and Joan was a waste of time and a bother, and you didn't like to have to listen to them talking all the way to work every day.
F1: Well, that's true sometimes, but today it was a real timesaver.
M1: Why? What happened?
F1: Well, you know how bad Friday afternoon rush-hour traffic can be, even without any problems. Well, today was a nightmare! There was a road crew doing construction work on the highway. . .
M1: Really?
F1: Yeah, the cars were backed up for miles. It was one of the worst traffic jams I've ever seen.
M1: So, how did you manage to get home early?
F1: If we hadn't been in the car pool lane, I'd still be stuck in traffic right now. All the traffic in the other lanes had to detour off the highway onto a little, two-lane road. But we just zipped along with no delays, and here I am—home early!

Picture Springboard: *Finish the conversation.*

F1: *(daughter)* Mama? Mama?
F2: What is it, honey?
F1: Are we going to get on the bus here?
F2: Yes, that's right, honey. This is a bus shelter, and it's where we get our bus.
F1: Are all the people here going to get on the bus?
F2: Uh-huh. Well, maybe not on our bus, but everybody's going to get on some bus.
F1: But what about that man in the wheelchair? How's he going to get on the bus?

F2: _____
F1: _____
M1 *(man in wheelchair)*: _____

LEARNING TO DRIVE (pp. 26–27)

Conversation Springboard: *What happened?*

M1: What's the matter, Bandar? You look like you just lost your best friend!
M2: Oh, hi, Kenji. No, I just failed the stupid road test for my driver license, that's all.
M1: That's too bad. What happened?
M2: I knocked over one of the cones parallel parking.
M1: You took a driver ed class, didn't you?
M2: Yeah, but I failed, anyway.
M1: Aw, don't worry about it. A lot of people fail the road test the first time, you know.
M2: Really? I don't know anybody else who did.
M1: My cousin had to retake the road test three times! The first time his steering wasn't so good, and he drove over the curb.
M2: Gee!
M1: The second time he forgot to look in the mirror before he backed up.
M2: Uh-oh. Did he hit anything?
M1: Yep. He backed right into a police car!
M2: Oh, no, you're kidding! So what happened the third time?
M1: By then the examiner was so nervous that she passed him just to get rid of him!
M2: Wow, I don't feel so bad now. I guess I'll go practice some more and take the test again.

Picture Springboard: *Finish the conversation.*

M3: All right, let's try the parallel parking again. Are you ready?
M2: I think so.
M3: See those two cones? They're the markers.
M2: OK, I see them.
M3: You have to park between them without touching either one. Think you can do that?

M2: _____
M3: _____
M2: _____

DRIVING PROBLEMS (pp. 28–29)

Conversation Springboard: *What's happening?*

M1: Hey, Mom! Look at that! That guy in front of us is going to lose his tailpipe!

F1: Do you think so? It does look a little wobbly.

M1: More than a little! It's hanging way down. If he goes over a bump, it'll hit the road for sure!

F1: I hope you're wrong, but I'm afraid you may be right, honey. The whole muffler looks really low.

M1: Well, do something, Mom. Beep the horn at him. I'll wave at him to pull over.
(beeps horn)

F1: I don't think he understood. He's speeding up! Oh, my gosh! It's scraping the road!

M1: You'd better slow down, Mom! It's going to fall off! Look out! (Muffler falls off car.)

F1: Oh, no! I don't believe it, I don't believe it! Right in the middle of the road!

M1: Good driving, Mom! I thought we were going to hit it for sure!

F1: I don't believe it! And he isn't even slowing down!

M1: I guess he doesn't even know what happened?

Picture Springboard: *Finish the conversation.*

F1: Just my luck! What a place for a flat tire, right in the middle of the desert! It's a good thing I'm prepared for it. . . Whew, it's hot! Boy, that's flat, all right. Now, let's see, where's the stuff to fix it . . . I think everything's in the trunk. (opens trunk) Yup. Here's the spare, and the jack. The lug wrench has to be here somewhere. Oh, there it is. That's everything. . . OK, now what do I do first? Hmm. . .

F1: _____

BUYING A CAR (pp. 30–31)

Conversation Springboard: *What's the process?*

M1: List car options, huh? Who wants to be the recorder. . . Nobody? Oh, come on, somebody has to do it. How about you, Miyako?

F1: I always have to do it! I think you guys expect me to do it just because I'm a woman. It's not fair!

M2: OK, OK, I'll do it. Just don't go too fast.

M1: All right, car options. Are there any in the vocabulary list?

M2: Yes, sun roof and bucket seats.

F1: And four-by-four, I think. I'm not exactly sure what that is.

M1: It's four-wheel drive. And, yes, it's optional. Can you think of any others?

M2: How about power options—power locks, power windows. . .

F1: And power brakes, power steering. . .

M1: I don't think power brakes and power steering are optional anymore. Don't all cars have them nowadays?

M2: Yes, I think so.

Teacher: OK, class, time's up. Let's see what you've got.

Picture Springboard: *Finish the conversation.*

M1: OK, here we are. Now remember, just let me do the talking.

F1: Oh, I don't trust these used car places at all! They always sell you a car with problems.

M2: Hi, there. Can I help you folks?

M1: _____

M2: _____

F1: _____

ON VACATION (pp. 32–33)

Conversation Springboard: *What's your opinion?*

F1: Hey, Oscar!

M1: Huh?

F1: Are you daydreaming? You look like you're a million miles away.

M1: Oh, this lesson on vacations got me started thinking about the kind of vacation I'd like to take, Mi Sook. . .

F1: I thought so. What is your dream vacation, Oscar?

M1: Well, you know I'm from The Dominican Republic. That's a beautiful tropical island in the Caribbean— like a paradise. I'd like to take my wife and kids back there for a vacation—stay in a beach house, lie in a hammock under the palm trees, with a big beach umbrella . . . That would be heavenly for me.

F1: Oh, Oscar, it sounds wonderful. You should do it!

M1: That's easier said than done. My wife and I have to work, and the children have school. It's hard to find the time and the money to do it. What about you, Mi Sook? What's your dream vacation?

F1: Mine's with my family, too. I haven't been back to Korea for more than a year, and I really miss my family. Sometimes I get so homesick that it's hard for me to study! I would love to just climb on a plane tomorrow, call my family from the airport in Seoul, and say, "Surprise, I'm home!"

M1: That sounds like an important vacation. I know you can't fly off tomorrow, but when *will* you be able to get back home to visit?

F1: I don't know. . .

Picture Springboard: *Finish the conversation.*

M1: Mmm, that's a beautiful travel brochure, Anita. Are you planning a trip to Germany?

F1: Yes, but not only Germany, Luigi. I love castles. I want to visit castles and cathedrals all over Europe! You're planning to go to Europe next summer, aren't you?

M1: Yes, with Mohammed. He's never been to Italy. We're going hiking in the Alps.

F1: Oh, that sounds like an adventure! Tell me more.

M1: _____

F1: _____

M1: _____

TRAVELING BY CAR (pp. 34–35)

Conversation Springboard: *What's happening?*

M1: Fill her up?
M2: Yes, and would you check the oil and radiator, too, please.
M1: Sure thing.
M2: We're not making very good time. The highway patrol's out in full force today. I've counted ten patrol cars in the past hour.
F1: Well, we don't want a speeding ticket, that's for sure.
F2: *(daughter)* Hey! Gimme that!
M3: *(son)* No! Let go of me! Mommy!
F2: You gimme that back! It's mine! Mom! *(Dog barks.)*
F1: Settle down, kids. Adriana, leave your brother alone.
F2: But he's got my earphones!
M3: No, they're mine!
F2: He broke his, and now he took mine!
F1: Tony, give your sister back the earphones. *(Dog barks again.)* How about it, kids. Let's take Cody for a walk on the grass over there. I think we all need a little rest!
F2: Not Grandpa. He's getting plenty of rest. He's been sleeping all day!

Picture Springboard: *Finish the conversation.*

M1: Honey?
F1: *(waking up)* Mmm... Oh. Where are we?
M1: At a motel just off the exit from the highway. I got too sleepy—had to stop for the night. The vacancy sign is on. I'll go in and register us for a room. *(grandfather snoring)*
F1: Just one room? I don't think we'll get much sleep with your father snoring all night!

M1: _____
F1: _____
M1: _____

BUS AND TRAIN TRAVEL (pp. 36–37)

Conversation Springboard: *What's next?*

M1: *(son)* Who was that man—the one that put our suitcases up there on the rack?
F1: That was the porter, honey.
M1: Can we eat on the train, Mommy?
F1: Yes, dear. They have a dining car, but we have some food with us, too. Are you hungry?
M1: No. When will we get to Washington, Mom?
F1: Tomorrow afternoon, dear.
M1: Where will we sleep tonight?
F1: Right here, dear. The seats fold down, and we can stretch out. They'll give us pillows and blankets.
M1: How come we can't sleep in a bed?
M2: Tickets, please.
F1: Oh, yes. Let's see now, where did I put those...
M1: We're going all the way to Washington to visit my grandma.
M2: Are you, now. That's a long trip.
M1: But Mommy says we're not sleeping in beds tonight. I saw a bed in a little room in that other car over there.
M2: Yes, that's a sleeper car. This is a coach.
F1: Honey, don't bother the conductor.
M2: Oh, that's all right, ma'am.
F1: I don't know what I did with those tickets... I had them right here...

Picture Springboard: *Finish the conversation.*

M1: May I help you, ma'am?
F1: Yes, please. Could you tell me what time it is here? The clocks say all different times, and I'm not sure what time zone I'm in anymore!
M1: It's 3:00 Mountain Standard Time.
F1: Oh, thank goodness! I was afraid I'd miss my train. Which track is the train to Chicago on, and how soon does it leave?

M1: _____
F1: _____
M1: _____

AIR TRAVEL (pp. 38–39)

Conversation Springboard: *What's happening?*

M1: Hi, can I help you with that?
F1: Thanks, I think I've got it now. This overhead compartment is kind of unusual.
M1: I think this is my seat. My ticket stub says 12A. Is that the window or the aisle seat?
F1: It's the aisle seat, but if you'd prefer the window, that's OK with me.
M1: Thanks, the aisle's fine with me.
M2: *(pilot's voice over PA system)* This is your captain. We are cleared for takeoff. Please make sure your seatbelts are securely fastened and all carry-on bags are stowed in the overhead compartments or under the seat in front of you. Flight attendants will be in the aisles to demonstrate safety equipment, and a safety manual is in the seat-back in front of you.
M1: Hmm... I can't find the other end of my seatbelt...
F1: Oh, sorry! I think I'm using it here! No wonder it didn't attach properly! Here you are. Now I wonder where the other part of mine is...
M1: I think you're sitting on it.
F1: Oh, for goodness sake, you're right! Thanks!

Picture Springboard: *Finish the conversation.*

M1: Can I take that for you, sir?
M2: Yes, thanks. I'm finished.
M1: Would you care for something more to drink?

M2: _____
M1: _____
M2: _____

UNIT 3: FINDING A JOB

JOBS IN YOUR COMMUNITY (pp. 42–45)

Conversation Springboard: *What's the process?*

F1: Do you think it'll be OK that we didn't all do this Community Activity together?
F2: It has to be OK, Mari! We couldn't go together!
M1: And we each did the activity. We probably got more information this way. What about you, Ilse? What did you find?
F2: Well, yesterday was such a beautiful day. I didn't want to waste the day doing homework. . .
M1: You mean you didn't do it?
F2: Oh, no, I did it, Tim. I did it in the park so I could enjoy the sunshine. I was surprised at how much was going on!
M1: Really? Not just some old people sitting on benches?
F2: No, not at all. A politician was there, giving a speech about saving the park. And there were reporters and cameras and police everywhere.
F1: Well, the "workplace" is easy—that's the park. What are those kinds of work?
F2: You mean the occupation categories from the vocabulary list? I didn't look them up yet.
M1: Here, look at the list. I think you saw communications, and government, and law enforcement, and news media, and photography. . .
F1: What about public service?
F2: You mean the politician? Yes, I guess so.
M1: That's good, Ilse. That's a lot.
F2: Oh, that's not all! There were lots of other people working in the park!

Picture Springboard: *Finish the conversation.*

F2: What place did you go to, Mari?
F1: Well, you know I'm awfully busy, so I really didn't have time to go anywhere special. . .
M1: Yes, but you always manage to do your assignments, Mari. I'm sure you found a way to do it.
F1: You're right, Tim. I did it on the bus on my way to work.
M1: On the bus? What did you see there?

F1: _____

F2: _____

F1: _____

YOUR OCCUPATION (pp. 46–47)

Conversation Springboard: *What's happening?*

M1: This should be a good lesson for the three of us since we all have jobs.
F1: That's true, Hector. What do you do?
M1: Well, I was an auto mechanic for years, Martine. Now I work in the special order department at the auto assembly plant.
F2: You work third shift, don't you, Hector?
M1: That's right. I go to work after class, work all night, and go to bed when the sun comes up!
F1: Doesn't that bother you? Staying up all night and sleeping in the daytime?

M1: Nope. I've always liked working at night.
F2: It sounds like you really enjoy your work, Hector.
M1: Yes, I do, Fatima. I really do. Don't you enjoy your job?
F2: Well, yes, in a way. I work as a hospital aide at City Hospital, and I do enjoy the contact with patients, but. . .
F1: I thought you were a doctor, Fatima.
F2: Yes, I am, and that's the problem. I was a doctor in my country, but I have to pass the English examinations for certification to practice medicine in this country, and that's really hard.
M1: Ah, I see. You're working as a hospital aide to get experience using all that medical vocabulary in English.
F2: That's right. And working with patients has really improved my English. The words patients use to tell how they're feeling aren't in any medical textbook.
F1: Like "feeling queasy," or "throwing up."
M1: Or being "under the weather" or "down in the dumps."
F2: Exactly. That's why I'm taking this conversation class.
F1: Good luck, Fatima! Pass that exam and we can all be your patients!

Picture Springboard: *Finish the conversation.*

M1: How about you, Martine? Do you like your job?
F1: Oh, I love it, Hector! It's part time, and that's perfect for me.
F2: What is your job, Martine? Tell us about it.

F1: _____

M1: _____

F1: _____

THE RIGHT JOB FOR YOU (pp. 48–49)

Conversation Springboard: *What's the process?*

F1: That was an interesting survey, Phong. Our ideal jobs are really different, aren't they?
M1: They sure are, Zelda. That's probably because *we're* pretty different.
F1: Yes, that's true. Let's see, now we have to report our partner's responses to another pair. Hey, Marcos, do you two want to do the reporting with us?
M2: Sure, Zelda. We're ready, right, Samara?
F2: Right. You guys go first, Phong.
M1: OK. The first question was "Which are more important to you in a job?" Then a lot of choices: "friendly co-workers," "a good supervisor," "good pay," etc. Zelda couldn't decide on that one.
F1: No, wait! That's not right, Phong! They're all important to me! We don't have to choose just one answer to that question. It says "Which are more important?" "Are" means more than one. And I care about all those things.
F2: Me, too, Zelda. That was my answer to the first question, too.
M2: How did Phong answer that question, Zelda?
F1: "Good pay" and "chance for advancement."

M1: Of course. That's what's more important. Sure, the other things are nice to have, but you have to admit, if the pay is bad and there's no chance for advancement, it's not a good job!
M2: I agree!
F1: I don't.
F2: Me, neither!

Picture Springboard: *Finish the conversation.*

M1: It's true, our company has had some pretty tough competition and some pretty heavy losses this past year. . .
F1: If anyone can pull our company out of this slump, it's you, John!
M1: Well, I look at this as a challenge for us all—an opportunity to show what our company can do! We're a team. With a little cooperation and our best efforts, we can be winners again!
M2: You know you can count on us, John. So, what's your plan?

M1: _____

F1: _____

M1: _____

LOOKING FOR A JOB (pp. 50–51)

Conversation Springboard: *What happened?*

F1: Did you ever find a job from a newspaper ad, Miki?
F2: No, Celia. Actually, I've never had a job.
F1: Really? Never? Not any kind of job?
F2: That's right. In my country, students study all the time. I never had time for a job. I was always too busy studying.
F1: And you're a good student, too, Miki. What about you, Luis? Have you ever found a job from a newspaper ad?
M1: Oh, sure, Celia. Newspaper ads, employment agencies, help wanted signs, word of mouth—you name it. I've tried them all.
F1: Sounds like you've had a lot of different jobs, Luis.
M1: That's true. I started working when I was a kid. I've lived in different places, and now I have four children, so I've been working for quite a while. But I've been lucky. I've always been able to find a job with no experience required.
F2: You must have a lot of experience by now!
M1: Yes, I guess I have. I've worked in restaurants and road construction and landscaping, and driving a taxi, and cleaning offices, and delivering pizzas. . . I even worked in a cemetery digging graves once!
F2: Oh, no! Why did you want to do that?
M1: I got that job by mistake. My English wasn't very good, and I thought the job was going to be landscaping.
F1: That must have been quite a surprise.
M1: Oh, yes. That's why I'm studying English. I don't want to make a mistake like that again!

Picture Springboard: *Finish the conversation.*

M1: Hi. I wonder if I could speak with the manager?
M2: Well, I'm the owner. Can I help you?

M1: I hope so. My name's Luis Rivera, and I saw your Help Wanted sign in the window.

M2: _____

M1: _____

M2: _____

APPLYING FOR A JOB (pp. 52–53)

Conversation Springboard: *What's next?*

F1: Um. . . Excuse me. . .
F2: Yes? What is it?
F1: Um. . . You asked me to fill in this form. . .
F2: The job application, yes. Is there a problem?
F1: Well, um, I'm not sure what to put here. . .
F2: What's that? Job experience? Just list the jobs you've had before.
F1: Um, yes, well. . .
F2: What did you say? Could you speak up, please?
F1: Yes. Sorry. I wonder if that means. . . well, does that mean any kind of work?
F2: Yes, any job you've ever had.
F1: Thank you. Um. . .
F2: Yes? Something else?
F1: No, no. . . I was just wondering whether. . . Well, could that maybe include volunteer work?
F2: You mean like the Red Cross? That kind of thing?
F1: Sort of. Like, helping out at home, maybe?

Picture Springboard: *Finish the conversation.*

F1: Hello, Mr. Rivera. Come right in. I'm Grace Chang. Here, have a seat.
M1: Thank you.
F1: I see from your application that you have a lot of job experience, Mr. Rivera.
M1: Well, I've had a number of different jobs over the years.
F1: Yes, and you have excellent references. Tell me, Mr. Rivera, what is particularly attractive to you about this job?

M1: _____

F1: _____

M1: _____

WAGES AND BENEFITS (pp. 54–55)

Conversation Springboard: *What's your opinion?*

F1: Do you think your new job will work out, Takeshi?
M1: I hope so, Izumi. It pays well. And it seems to have a good benefits package.
F1: What benefits are there?
M1: Well, it has really good group health insurance, with complete medical and hospitalization coverage.
F1: So, if we have another baby, that will be covered?
M1: Right. They even have family leave. And we can go to any doctor or any hospital we want!
F1: Is there dental coverage? I know Hiroshi's teeth are going to need braces.
M1: Yes, there's a dental plan. And eye coverage, too. Michiyo can get a new pair of glasses free every year.
F1: Oh, wonderful. Health care is so expensive in this country. I'm glad we won't have to worry about it! What about vacation time for you, Takeshi?
M1: Well, I'll get two weeks of paid vacation every year, plus eleven paid holidays. And six paid sick days.
F1: Well, you won't need those. You never get sick.
M1: I hope not, but it's good to have them, anyway. There's life insurance, too, and a retirement plan.
F1: Oh, Takeshi, it does sound wonderful! We'll be well taken care of.
M1: It looks that way, Izumi. I just hope I like the job now.
F1: You will, don't worry. It sounds perfect!

Picture Springboard: *Finish the conversation.*

F2: If that's all clear, Mr. Suzuki, and you understand this employment contract, then you just need to sign the agreement right here, at the bottom.
M1: Actually, I do have one question.
F2: Well, now's the time to ask. I'll do my best to answer. What's your question, Mr. Suzuki?
M1: _____
F2: _____
M1: _____

UNIT 4: LIFE AT WORK

STARTING A NEW JOB (pp. 58–59)

Conversation Springboard: *What's next?*

M1: Good morning. I'm Tom Rogers. You must be Angela Soulas, our new data entry clerk.
F1: Yes, I am. I'm pleased to meet you, Mr. Rogers.
M1: Oh, just call me Tom—everyone does.
F1: OK. And most people call me Angie.
M1: Well, Angie, this is it—the R & D Data Entry Department. Welcome to the group. You'll get acquainted with everyone here pretty quickly. This is Ellen Grant, Viv Russell, Amy Wang, Dan Long, and Bob Fellows back at the copy machine. Everyone, this is Angie Soulas.
Group: Hi, Angie. Welcome. Glad to have you.
F1: Hi.

M1: Amy will show you how to handle the data entry you'll be working on, and Viv will show you how to handle our complicated copy machine.
M2: That copier has a mind of its own.
F2: That copier works just fine if you treat it right!
M2: Only for you, Viv!
F2: Hmph!
M1: And here's your desk, Angie. I'll leave you in Amy's capable hands now. If there's anything that's unclear or that you're confused about, don't be embarrassed to ask. Amy knows everything about the data programs we use.
F1: Thanks, Mr. Rogers... Oh, sorry... Tom. Looks like I'll be just fine.

Picture Springboard: *Finish the conversation.*

F1: *(to herself)* Let's see, how did Viv say to start this copier? I think she said you have to restart it each time... She explained it so fast that I don't remember what she said. Impatient people make me nervous. I'm always afraid I'll make an error... Hmm... Maybe it's this green button... Yes, I think this must be it... *(Copier jams.)* Oh, no!
F2: What are you doing there! Oh...
F1: _____
F2: _____
F1: _____

INSTRUCTIONS AT WORK (pp. 60–61)

Conversation Springboard: *What's happening?*

M1: Aha! Roman and Liz, hard at work! How are you two doing with those building modifications?
M2: Not so well, Andrew. This new software isn't very friendly. Right now it's just giving us a bunch of garbage.
F1: You've worked with it, Andrew. What do you think could be wrong? Could you give us a hand?
M1: I'd like to, but I'm on my way to a big meeting, and I'll be tied up for the rest of the day. Here's the software manual. I'm sure you won't have any serious problems.
F1: We've already got serious problems.
M1: Oh, it's probably just something minor. Double check the instructions in the manual again. And remember, these modifications have to be done today!
F1: Right. Have a good meeting, Andrew.
M2: Yes, have fun.
M1: You, too. See you tomorrow.
F1: Well, that's great. "Check the manual," he says.
M2: We'll be here all night at this rate, while he's out on the golf course.
F1: The golf course! I thought he had a big meeting.
M2: That's where they have their big meetings—on the golf course!

Picture Springboard: *Finish the conversation.*
(waitress and customers in restaurant)

M1: I'll have the taco special—and does that come with chips and salsa?

F1: It comes with rice and beans, but I can bring you some chips and salsa if you'd like. . .
F2: Excuse me. Would you change my salad dressing to Italian, please? I think I ordered ranch—or was it French?
M2: Miss? I'd like to order an appetizer. . .
M1: Hold it, everybody! We're going to confuse this poor waitress. Let's try this one at a time! You first, Lucy.
F2: OK, Jim. Sorry. . .
F2: _____
F1: _____
M2: _____

DOING A GOOD JOB (pp. 62–63)

Conversation Springboard: *What's your opinion?*

F1: These are beautiful strawberries, Mr. Garcia. I'll have to buy some for my mom.
M1: Yes, they *are* nice, Katie. Have you seen Melanie this morning?
F1: No, I haven't.
M1: Hmph!
F2: Oh, hi, Mr. Garcia. Hi, Katie.
F1: Hi, Melanie.
M1: Hmph. Let's get these strawberries ready and out front. They're our big produce special today, and everybody's going to want them.
F2: OK, OK, don't worry—we'll have them out there in plenty of time. Right, Katie. . .
M1: Hmm. Well, get to work now, and I want to talk with you later, Melanie. Stop by my office on your break.
F2: What's bothering him? The man is such a grouch!
F1: Well, he's the manager, Melanie. And you're late again.
F2: Oh, great! You're on my case, too! You sound like I'm late every day.
F1: Well, you *are* late a lot.
F2: Mmm. . . beautiful strawberries, aren't they! *(eats one)* Delicious, too! I didn't have time for breakfast, but these will do just fine. Have some, Katie.
F1: We shouldn't be eating them, Melanie. They're for the customers.
F2: Oh, Katie, you're too good. Mmm. . . These *are* good!

Picture Springboard: *Finish the conversation.*

F1: Here's your change, ma'am, and your receipt. Have a nice day.
F2: Oh, dear, what's she doing to my groceries?!
F1: I beg your pardon. . .
F2: The bag is tearing!
F3: What?
F1: _____
F2: _____
F3: _____

INJURIES AT WORK (pp. 64–65)

Conversation Springboard: *What happened?*

F1: Hi, Henry. How're you feeling?
M1: Oh, hi, Jane. I've been better. Where am I?
F1: You're in the hospital.
M1: What happened? How'd I get here? Who are you?
F2: I'm Dr. Latham. You don't remember anything?
M1: No. The last I remember, I was in the lab, working with the XF2 compound. Did I faint? Oh, my head hurts!
F1: No, Henry, you didn't faint. The beaker exploded!
M1: An explosion? That's impossible! We took every precaution.
F1: Well, something went wrong, that's for sure. Those chemicals are highly combustible—you know that. And the fumes are poisonous.
M1: Oh, boy. So, what's my condition, Doctor? Am I going to be all right?
F2: Well, you have a concussion from the explosion, and there's some damage to your lungs from the fumes, but you're going to be OK. You're a lucky man!
M1: Lucky. . . Is everybody else OK? What about the experiment?
F1: Everybody else is fine. And don't worry about the lab, Henry.
F2: That's right. You need to get some rest now. You can talk again later.

Picture Springboard: *Finish the conversation.*

F1: OK, now, Mrs. Delaney. I'm just going to lift you out of the bed and help you into the wheelchair.
F2: I'm pretty heavy for a little thing like you to lift. . .
F1: Oh, don't worry, I do this all the time. Ready now? Lift! Oh! Oh, no!

F2: _____
F1: _____
F2: _____

DEDUCTIONS FROM PAY (pp. 66–67)

Conversation Springboard: *What's the process?*

M1: Oh, a Class Survey. OK, let's start with Bill and Dorina. Did either of you ever have Medicare tax or Social Security contributions deducted from your income?
M2: Sure!
F1: Of course. Everybody does.
M2: Right. You don't have any choice about those deductions. They're required.
M1: For part-time work, too?
F1: I think so.
F2: Well, nobody ever deducts those from my pay when I baby-sit.
M1: And when I mow lawns for people, they pay me in cash. They never deduct anything.
F1: I think they're supposed to, or you're supposed to, or something...
F2: Do you know, Bill?
M2: No, I'm not sure about that, either. But we could find out.
F2: Really? How?
M2: There's a toll-free number to call with tax questions. It's listed in the phone directory.
F1: Or we could just ask the teacher. He'll know.
M1: I'm not sure I want to find out...

Picture Springboard: *Finish the conversation.*

F1: Oh, Rosa, I got my first paycheck, but something's wrong! I don't understand what happened. Can you help me?
F2: I'll try, Paula. What doesn't seem right?
F1: Well, my earnings say $320, but they've only paid me $211.90. It has to be a mistake!
F2: May I see it? Hmm... It looks OK to me, Paula.
F1: But, that's impossible! It's so little money!

F2: _____
F1: _____
F2: _____

SPENDING MONEY (pp. 68–69)

Conversation Springboard: *What's your opinion?*

F1: What a perfect day!
M1: Mmm... and great chicken!
F1: Well, chicken was on sale this week.
M1: That's my wife, always economizing.
F1: I just don't like to waste money. And there's something special about simple pleasures. A picnic in the country, blue sky, sunshine, Tony chasing butterflies... Tony, don't go too far!
M2: OK, Mama.
M1: I'm glad you're a sensible woman, Lupita.
F1: Thanks, Roberto. That reminds me—I'm really worried about Costas.
M1: The guy at your office? What did he do now?
F1: Well, he has a new girlfriend, and you know how extravagant he is, always splurging on something.
M1: Oh, yes, I remember—only the best for Costas. So, what's he doing to impress his new girlfriend?

F1: Well, he bought a new car—one of those fancy sports cars—and he's been taking her out to expensive nightclubs and restaurants. Costas and I make the same amount of money, and I know if you and I were spending money that way, we'd go broke pretty fast.
M1: Well, don't worry too much, Lupita. There's nothing you can do about it. Costas is just going to have to learn the hard way.
F1: Yes, I guess you're right. I'm glad you're not like that, Roberto. Want some more chicken?

Picture Springboard: *Finish the conversation.*

M3: Wait a minute... What's this? Oh, no! I don't believe it!
F1: What's the matter, Costas?
M3: A repossession notice! They want to repossess my new car! What will Kiki say? We're supposed to go dancing tonight! They can't do that!

F1: _____
M3: _____
F1: _____

PAYING TAXES (pp. 70–71)

Conversation Springboard: *What's next?*

M1: What's the matter, Nick?
M2: I'm pretty worried, Mattiew. I just got a letter yesterday saying that my taxes are being audited!
M1: Do you have any idea why?
M2: No, not at all! I don't think I made any errors in computing...
M1: Generally, when they audit somebody's taxes, it's because they found something unusual.
M2: I can't think of anything unusual about mine. I didn't have any unusual income; I took a standard deduction; I don't have any dependents or exemptions or tax credits; and I filed my return on time.
M1: What bad luck!
M2: That's for sure. I don't know much about tax audits, but I do know the taxpayer always loses!
M1: That's why I have an accountant do my taxes, Nick. I was audited once when I moved from one state to another. The auditor said I owed money—and, of course, a late penalty, too!
M2: Oh, boy! Maybe I should talk to your accountant. Is he any good?
M1: It's a she, Linda Ross, and yes, I think she's a good tax accountant. She might be able to help you. Here's her number. Good luck!
M2: Thanks, Mattiew. I'm afraid I'll need it.

Picture Springboard: *Finish the conversation.*

F1: You look really happy, Mai.
F2: Oh, I am, Diana! I just got my tax refund check!
F1: Refund? What's that?
F2: They withheld too much from my income last year, and now they're giving it back to me.
F1: Oh, dear, I don't understand these tax forms at all. What's a W-2? or a 1040EZ? or a Standard

Deduction? I mean, I haven't even filed yet! What do I have to do? Can you and Mina help me?
F2: Oh, Mina knows a lot more about it than I do.
F3: _____
F1: _____
F3: _____

LEAVING A JOB (pp. 72–73)

Conversation Springboard: *What's your opinion?*

M1: Hmm. . . I like the questions for this Partner Interview, Ruth. They look interesting.
F1: I think so, too, Kien. Let me ask you first. "Have you ever left a job? Why or why not?"
M1: Yes, I've left jobs for a lot of reasons—low pay, career change, seasonal layoffs, poor working conditions, moving to another city. . .
F1: That *is* a lot of reasons, Kien. "Would you keep a bad job if you really needed the money?"
M1: Well, I did that once. It was just after our first child was born. My wife and I didn't have any money to pay the doctor or buy clothes for the baby. The job I had then was washing dishes in a restaurant—long hours, very low pay; my boss was *always* in a bad mood, and she even once accused me of stealing from her! I wanted to leave that job so badly, but I stayed.
F1: Are you sorry you stayed?
M1: No, I've never regretted staying, Ruth. We needed the money, and I didn't speak much English then.
F1: Would you do it again?
M1: I hope I never have to!
F1: I hope not, too, Kien. What about the last two questions: "What makes a job good?" and "What makes a job bad?"
M1: Those are easy questions for me, Ruth. If you like a job, it's good. If you don't, it's bad.

Picture Springboard: *Finish the conversation.*

M1: We'll be sorry to lose you, Teresa. I'm really going to miss you. You're a beautiful woman, you know. . .
F1: Well, Bob, I'm sorry, too. There are a lot of things I like about this job, but I simply can't continue working here.
M1: Why not, Teresa? Everybody loves you! And you know how I feel. Why do you insist on leaving?
F1: Well, Bob, if you really want to know, I'll tell you. You know I'm a married woman, and you know I'm not interested in having a personal relationship with you, but you keep making improper advances. I've asked you to stop, but you don't. I'm really tired of it, so I'm leaving!
M1: _____
F1: _____
M1: _____

UNIT 5: IN THE NEWS

CLASS NEWS (pp. 76–77)

Conversation Springboard: *What happened?*

F1: Question One: Who has had the best week? How has your week been, Van?
M1: Terrible! I don't want to talk about it. I'm sure everybody else's week has been better than mine!
M2: No, mine's been terrible, too.
F1: I bet it hasn't been as bad as mine!
F2: Or mine. It sounds as though we've all had a bad week.
M2: Maybe we should start with Question Two instead: Who has had the worst week?
F1: Good idea. My car was stolen on Monday. The police found it Wednesday, but it was a mess. I'm not sure I can even get it repaired!
F2: Oh, that's too bad, Mayra!
M2: It is too bad, but my week was still worse.
F1: Really? What happened to you, Norm?
M2: My wife left me.
F1, F2, M1: Oh, dear, how awful! I'm really sorry. That's terrible, Norm!
F1: But maybe she'll come back.
M2: I doubt it.
F2: I guess my week hasn't been so bad after all. I've just had too much work to do.
M2: What about you, Van? You said your week was too terrible to talk about. Do you still feel that way?
M1: I'm afraid so.
F1: Hey, what's happening? It looks like two immigration officers are outside our classroom door. I wonder what's wrong.
M1: Uh-oh. Time to say goodbye.
F2: Goodbye? Where are you going, Van?
M1: Sorry, Emi, you'll have to read about it in the news. So long, guys!
F1, F2, M2: Oh, no! Oh, Van! What on earth. . .

Picture Springboard: *Finish the conversation.*

F1: OK, who has some personal news for the next class newsletter?
F2, M1, M2: I do. I have some. Me, too!
F1: I have some, too. This is going to be a good newsletter! Who wants to take notes?
F2: I can't. I'm right-handed, and look at my arm! That's my news.
M1: I'll do it. I need the practice. OK, Yana, you first. Tell us about your arm. What happened?
F2: _____
F1: _____
M1: _____
M2: _____

109

NEWS MEDIA (pp. 78–79)

Conversation Springboard: *What's your opinion?*

(telephone conversation)

F1: Good evening. I'm calling from WKGB radio. I'd like to speak with the lady of the house, if I may.
M1: That's my mom. Sorry, she's busy right now.
F1: Is your father at home now?
M1: Yes, but he's busy, too. Can I take a message?
F1: We're conducting a survey of people's news preferences at WKGB. May I ask, are you an adult member of the household?
M1: Well, I'm in high school.
F1: And would you be willing to answer a few questions regarding your family's news preferences?
M1: Well, yes, I guess so.
F1: Fine. Does anyone in the household watch news on television?
M1: Yes, that's what my parents are doing right now.
F1: Oh, fine. And does anyone read a daily newspaper?
M1: Yes, my dad does, every day.
F1: Does anyone read a weekly newsmagazine?
M1: My mom does.
F1: And what is *your* personal preference for news?
M1: I get sports news on-line on my computer. That's what I was doing when you called.
F1: I'm sorry I interrupted you. Just one more question. Does anyone in the household listen to WKGB radio news?
M1: Oh, yeah. My dad sets his radio alarm so that he wakes up to the six o'clock news every morning. I guess you could say our family likes to keep up on the news.
F1: That's for sure! Thanks for your cooperation.

Picture Springboard: *Finish the conversation.*

F1: Congratulations, Governor. This is a big victory for you.
F2: Can you tell us how you're feeling right now?
M1: Wonderful!
F2: Do you have anything you'd like to say to our television viewers at this time?
M1: _____
F1: _____
M1: _____

WEATHER AND NATURAL DISASTERS (pp. 80–81)

Conversation Springboard: *What happened?*

F1: What about this last question, "Who has experienced a natural disaster?"
F2: I have. When I was a little girl, a terrible hurricane struck The Dominican Republic. It was just awful! The roof blew off our house. And my cousin's whole house was blown away.
F1: Oh, no!
F2: I still have nightmares about the howling wind. I really thought we were all going to die. A lot of people did die.
M1: That's how I felt when my town in Japan was destroyed by an earthquake, Celia. It was so terrifying! Buildings collapsed everywhere. The whole block where we lived was nothing but rubble!
M2: How did you escape, Yukio?
M1: We were just lucky, Will. My sister and I were at home, and we rushed outside as soon as the ground started shaking. Our house collapsed behind us.
F2: How terrible! Where did you go? What did you do?
M1: Well, the International Red Cross helped us—they gave all the people blankets and food. And then our parents sent us away to stay with our uncle.
F1: What about you, Will?
M2: I've never experienced a natural disaster, Connie, and I hope I never do.
F1: Me, too. Watching them on the news and listening to Celia and Yukio tell about them is bad enough!

Picture Springboard: *Finish the conversation.*

M1: Here you go, Miss. You want to hand me the cat first?
F1: She's afraid of the water! She won't let go. . .
M1: OK, I've got her. . . Let me give you a hand now.
F1: Oh, thank you!
M1: I thought we evacuated everybody last night. Another ten minutes and the water will be over the top of that roof! How come you're still here?
F1: _____
M1: _____
F1: _____

SPORTS NEWS (pp. 82–83)

Conversation Springboard: *What's the process?*

M1: These Vocabulary Challenges are really hard for me. I can never think of vocabulary fast.
F1: Neither can I, Kuo Hsiu. And especially this one. I don't know any sports well.
M1: Well, I know a lot of sports vocabulary in Mandarin and Cantonese, but I don't know much in English.
F1: I guess it's all up to you then, Manny. What sport do you know well?
M2: Oh, baseball, I guess. A lot of the words are similar in Spanish.
M1: Good. I do know a few words for baseball.
F1: OK, I'll be the recorder. At least I can spell pretty well. What are some words?
M1: Bat, ball, glove, base. And what do they call the one who throws the ball?
M2: The pitcher. And the catcher catches. The ones hitting the ball are the batters. The other players are first baseman, second baseman, third baseman. . .
F1: And fourth baseman? There are four bases, aren't there?
M2: Yes, but the fourth base is called home plate. That's where the catcher stands and the batters bat.
M1: Aren't the players who chase the ball called outfielders?

M2: Yes. But there's one other player we haven't mentioned who plays in closer, between second and third base. That one's the short stop.
F1: Short stop, OK. What about the ones who wave their arms and say, "You're out!"
M2: Those aren't players, Irini. They're the umpires.
M1: Yeah, they control the game. And the ones who run up to the umpires and shout at them? Who are they?
M2: Those are the managers.
Teacher: All right, class, time's up. Let's have the reports.

Picture Springboard: *Finish the conversation.*

M1: And now for a recap of today's international sports events.
F1: The Ukrainians are still leading in the world amateur mixed-pairs figure skating competition.
M1: In Sweden, at the track and field games, Mexico won a gold medal in the pole vault.
F1: There was big news in the soccer finals today, and surprises in two other events. Tell us about them, Greg.

M1: _____
F1: _____
M1: _____

ENTERTAINMENT NEWS (pp. 84–85)

Conversation Springboard: *What's your opinion?*

M1: Where in the newspaper would entertainment be listed?
M2: Sometimes there's an "entertainment" section. Check the "contents" on the front page.
F1: This paper has movies on one page and sports in another section...
F2: And an "upcoming events" section with other kinds of entertainment. Oh, look at this one! The Boston Fine Arts Chamber Music Trio is performing music of Bach and Mozart on violin, viola, and cello tonight at 8:00. Doesn't that sound wonderful?
M1: Well, I'm not too fond of classical music, Florence. This one sounds better to me: Cochise County Fair and Rodeo, Saturday and Sunday. I love county fairs and rodeos. How about it?
F1: Hmm... maybe. What do you guys think of this one? Open-air art show—"Art in the Park"—featuring crafts and paintings by well-known area artists. Maybe I could find something nice to buy there.
M2: Oh, wait! Listen to this; this is definitely the best! Grand opening! Karchner Caverns opens to the public after ten years of preparation! Caves never seen before! Now that's really a big event!
F2: I still like the chamber music concert best.
F1: And I like the "Art in the Park."
M1: I guess I'm the only one who wants to see the rodeo and county fair, huh?
M2: And the rest of you don't seem very interested in the caverns.
F2: I wonder if the other groups are doing any better than we are...

Picture Springboard: *Finish the conversation.*

M1: OK, kids. Where would you like to go for Suzie's birthday? How about a country music show?
M2: Nah... Wow! Look at this, Dad. Mario the Magnificent! I saw him on TV. He's a really famous magician. He does amazing tricks. And we could see him in person!
M1: How does that sound to you, Suzie? It's your birthday. Would you like to go see Mario the Magnificent?

F1: _____
M2: _____
M1: _____

CRIME IN THE NEWS (pp. 86–87)

Conversation Springboard: *What's your opinion?*

M1: Hi. I wonder if you two would mind answering a question for me.
F1: That depends. What's it for?
M1: My class is doing a school survey on capital punishment.
F1: The death penalty, huh? OK, what's the question?
M1: Do you approve of capital punishment?
F1: Well, that depends.
M1: You mean you're not sure? You can say, "yes," "no," or "not sure."
F1: No, I'm sure. It depends on how bad the crime is. If somebody does something really terrible, then, yes, I do approve of capital punishment.
M1: OK, thanks. You say "yes."
F1: Yes, I approve in certain cases.
F2: Well, I don't agree with her. I don't think killing another person is ever OK.
M1: So your answer is "no."
F2: That's right. I'm against it.
M1: OK. Thank you both. I appreciate your comments.
F2: No problem.
F1: Good luck with your survey.

Picture Springboard: *Finish the conversation.*

M1: ... Now, Mrs. Moya, I'm going to ask you to look around this courtroom very carefully and tell me if you see that man here today.
F1: Yes, I do. It's him—that man right over there, sitting at that table.
M1: Are you sure of that, Mrs. Moya?
F1: Oh, yes, very sure. It was in the daytime, and I was only a few feet away.
M1: Thank you. Now, Mrs. Moya, would you tell the jury exactly what you saw that day?

F1: _____
M1: _____
F1: _____

HEROES IN THE NEWS (pp. 88–89)

Conversation Springboard: *What's your opinion?*

F1: Who's your personal hero, Jack?
M1: My father was always my personal hero, Jeanine.
F1: That's great, Jack! What did you admire about him?
M1: Well, he wasn't famous, and he wasn't especially big, or rich, or powerful, but he was something a lot more important than those things to me.
F1: In what ways?
M1: He was my ideal of what a father should be—of what a man should be. He worked hard, he believed in himself, he believed in me. He always knew what was important in life. He never made excuses, he seldom complained, and he never backed down from something he believed was right.
F1: He sounds like a wonderful man, Jack. I can see why he's your hero.
M2: Who's your personal hero, Jeanine?
F1: Oh, I've had a lot of personal heroes, Andy. Right now the one I admire the most is Mother Teresa. Her life was so remarkable! It really inspires me. She was just a tiny nun from Albania who wanted to help the poor, and she started over 500 missions in more than 100 countries!
M1: Yes, Mother Teresa was an extraordinary person. What about you, Andy? Who's your personal hero?
M2: I don't think I have one. I just don't think that way. Yes, there are lots of good people who do great things, but I just don't think of any of them as my own personal hero.

Picture Springboard: *Finish the conversation.*

F1: This is the Lincoln Memorial, Johnny.
M1: And that big statue is Abraham Lincoln, isn't it?
F1: Yes, it is. Now look at the penny. What do you see?
M1: The face on the penny looks like the face on the statue.
F1: That's right, honey. What do you know about Abraham Lincoln?
M1: _____
F1: _____
M1: _____

LOCAL NEWS (pp. 90–91)

Conversation Springboard: *What's the process?*

M1: Rosa and Sungjoon, would you be our recorders for this Class Brainstorm? Just write all the ideas on the board.
M2: OK. Write everything?
M1: Yes, all the ideas. You write all the local problems and issues on the left side, Sungjoon. And, Rosa, you can write all the good news on the right side.
F1: OK, I'm ready.
M1: Now, let's brainstorm everybody. What are some local problems and issues? Any ideas?
F2: How about car theft? A lot of people have their cars stolen.
M2: Graffiti. Gangs!
F1: Overcrowded schools!
F2: Pollution.
M1: Any more? No? Well, what about good news?
F2: Hmm. . . That's harder to think of. . .
M1: Why is that? There are good things about our community, aren't there?
M2: Yes, but it's easier to think of bad things. . .
M1: Well, how about this—the Thunder Mountain Scuba Club is cleaning up Parker Lake to make it safer for swimmers.
F1: That's a good one. I'm putting it down.
F2: How about the new job the city just created—"Neighborhood Officer"—to enforce the illegal dumping laws?
M2: And the 100 new computers that the employees at Micro Technology donated to our school district?
F2: And the after-school city art program—the kids are painting over graffiti and making beautiful murals.
F1: I've seen some of them. They're great! You know, once we get started, it's not so hard to think of good news.
M2: Yes, that's a relief!

Picture Springboard: *Finish the conversation.*

F1: What a beautiful day!
M1: It sure is, Daria.
F1: The forest always smells so clean and fresh. I love to be able to get out and hike like this, away from all the noise and pollution of the city. . .
M1: Oh, my! Unbelievable!
F1: What's that truck doing, Mike?
M1: _____
F1: _____
M1: _____

WORLD NEWS (pp. 92–93)

Conversation Springboard: *What's your opinion?*

M1: Now we have to list current world problems. That should be easy.
F1: It's true. There are so many. Where do we start?
M2: Anywhere, I guess. How about famine and overpopulation and war. . .
F2: And terrorists and refugees and starvation. . .
M1: And natural disasters! So many people have died this year from floods and earthquakes. . .
F1: And that awful volcanic eruption that destroyed half of an island. . .
F2: And those two airplane crashes that killed so many people. . .
M1: And that big oil spill that destroyed hundreds of miles of coastline, wiping out all kinds of fish and wildlife. . .
M2: And don't forget disease—all the people dying of AIDS, and the cholera epidemic, and what's the name of that new virus?
F1: Oh, this is really depressing! I don't like doing this. It makes me think that the world is in really bad shape!
M1: Well, it is, Jill. Face it, our world is in big trouble!
F2: Oh, Wally, you're such a pessimist.
M2: I don't think so, Kris. I think he's a realist.

M1: Right! We've got two choices: We can either hide our heads in the sand like ostriches, or we can face the problems and do something about them!

Picture Springboard: *Finish the conversation.*

F1: ... And so at this time the fighting continues... In health news tonight, researchers announced today a major breakthrough in a different kind of fight—the battle against the deadly AIDS virus. Mark Britton has the story for us.

M1: Here at the HIV Research Institute in Chicago, an exciting discovery was announced today by AIDS researchers Paul Moreno and Libby Poe. Dr. Poe, can you tell us about this new discovery?

F2 *(Dr. Poe)*: _____

M1 *(M. Britton)*: _____

M2 *(Dr. Moreno)*: _____

POLITICS AND GOVERNMENT IN THE NEWS (pp. 94–95)

Conversation Springboard: *What's your opinion?*

F1: It's hard to believe that this is our last Find Someone Who activity.

F2: I know. The semester has gone by so fast. Do you think my English sounds better than it did at the start of the semester?

F1: Much better, Young Hee. What about mine?

F2: Oh, your English always sounded good to me, Ivana.

F1: Really? Thanks, Young Hee.

M1: Hey, you guys. This is supposed to be a Find Someone Who about politics.

F1: Well, I'm not very interested in politics, Cesar.

F2: Me, neither.

M1: You mean you don't vote?

F1: Well, where I live now, I'm not eligible to vote.

M1: Oh. How about you, Young Hee? Are you interested in politics?

F2: Sometimes, Cesar... when there's an issue I care about. I participated in a protest against nuclear weapons once.

M1: That sounds interesting. What happened? Did you get arrested?

F2: No, it was a big protest. The police couldn't arrest everyone, so they ended up not arresting anybody.

F1: Why are you so interested in politics, Cesar?

M1: Well, I think you have to be, Ivana. All of us do. Other people are interested, you know. And if we don't pay attention, and we don't care, then we'll just be stuck with whatever those other people want. And that's not good enough for me.

F2: Maybe you should go into politics, Cesar. I'd vote for you!

F1: Me, too, Cesar. You really should!

Picture Springboard: *Finish the conversation.*

F1: This is Channel 5 reporting live from campaign headquarters, where the winning candidate, Louis Robinson, is about to make his victory speech...

M1: Thank you, thank you! My wife and I want to thank you all for your support. Tonight we celebrate *your* victory! And tonight I pledge to you that I will keep each and every one of the campaign promises I have made! *Every* one! And what are those promises? You tell me!

F2 *(woman in crowd)*: _____

M2 *(man in crowd)*: _____

GRAMMAR FOR CONVERSATION CONTENTS

UNIT 1: HOUSING
Word Families *(decorate-decoration-decorative-decoratively)*
Passive/Active Tenses *(The yard is being fenced./They are fencing the yard.)*
Passive/Active Modals *(The house might be sold./They might sell the house.)*
A person who/groups which/questions that

UNIT 2: TRANSPORTATION AND TRAVEL
Word Families *(commute-commuter-commuting)*
Advantage of taking/disadvantage of commuting/ reason for carpooling
It takes a long time to get there
Time Clauses *(before/when/after he fails the test)*
Do you think/Do you know/I don't know/Could you tell me
The first time (that) you drove
re- [again]

UNIT 3: FINDING A JOB
Word Families *(apply-application-applied)*
-ment, -tion
To be willing + Infinitive
Passive Voice *(What training is required?)*
Noun Clauses *(An advantage is that)*
Modals *(What could/would/should he do?)*
-al

UNIT 4: LIFE AT WORK
Word Families *(stress-stress-stressful-stressfully)*
dis-, im-, in-, ir-, un-
It's confusing/I'm confused
-ful [with]/-less [without]
-able, -ent, -eous, -ible, -ic, -ical, -ious, -ive, -ous, -tious, -y)
-sion, -tion
How to, when to, where to, which to, what to, whether to

UNIT 5: IN THE NEWS
Word Families *(compete-competition-competitive-competitively)*
Word Families *(newscast, newspaper)*
The fireman who rescued them
The reporter interviewing people
Passive Voice *(Who will be affected? The boy was shot.)*

GRAMMAR FOR CONVERSATION

UNIT 1

WORD FAMILIES

Verb	Noun	Adjective	Adverb
afford		affordable	affordably
collect	collection/collector	collective	collectively
	convenience	convenient	conveniently
decorate	decoration/decorator	decorative	decoratively
distrust	distrust/distrustfulness	distrustful	distrustfully
maintain	maintenance	maintained	
notify	notification	notifiable	
organize	organization/organizer	organizational	organizationally
rehabilitate	rehabilitation	rehabilitated	
renovate	renovation	renovated	
rent	rent/renter	rental/rentable	
vandalize	vandalism/vandal	vandalized	

PASSIVE & ACTIVE VOICE (Comparison of Tenses)

Passive

Present:	Everyone	is satisfied	with this solution.
Present Progressive:	The yard	is being fenced.	
Past:	Their house	was insured	against fire and theft.
Past Progressive:	Their house	was being remodeled.	
Future:	His telephone service	will be discontinued.	
Present Perfect:	The roof	has been damaged	by the storm.

Active

Present:	This solution	satisfies	everyone.
Present Progressive:	They	are fencing	the yard.
Past:	They	insured	their house and belongings.
Past Progressive:	They	were remodeling	their house.
Future:	The phone company	will discontinue	his telephone service.
Present Perfect:	The storm	has damaged	the roof.

PASSIVE & ACTIVE (Comparison of Modal Auxiliaries)
Passive

Can:	Most utility problems	can be avoided	with this solution.
Could:	This room	could be painted	easily.
May:	Some utilities	may be cut off	for non-payment.
Might:	The house	might be sold	by next week.
Should:	That neighborhood	should be improved.	
Must:	The bank says our house	must be insured.	

PASSIVE & ACTIVE (Comparison of Modal Auxiliaries)
Active

Can:	People	can avoid	most utility problems.
Could:	Someone	could paint	this room easily.
May:	Some utility companies	may cut off	service for non-payment.
Might:	They	might sell	the house by next week.
Should:	Someone	should improve	that neighborhood.
Must:	The bank says we	must insure	our house.

ADJECTIVE CLAUSES (*Who/Which/That* as subjects)

Who:	Describe a person	who	is a good neighbor.
Which:	Are there groups	which	are improving your community?
That:	Write questions	that	are important to ask.

UNIT 2

WORD FAMILIES

Verb	Noun	Adjective	Adverb
collide	collision	colliding	
commute	commute/commuter	commuting	
experience	experience	experienced/experiential	
intoxicate	intoxication	intoxicated/intoxicating	
negotiate	negotiation/negotiator	negotiable	
renew	renewal	renewed/renewable	
restrict	restriction	restrictive/restricted	

Advantages of/Disadvantages of/Reasons for + gerund

What are the	advantages of taking	a bus or a train to work?
What are some	disadvantages of commuting	a long distance to work?
What are some good	reasons for carpooling?	

It takes + infinitive

Question

How much time	does it take to renew	your license?
How long	did it take to drive	to work today?
How many hours	will it take to get	there?

Answer

It takes	a long time!
It took	twenty minutes.
It will take	three hours.

TIME CLAUSES (*Before/After/When*)

Before:	What does the man do **before he takes the driving test**?
	Before he takes the driving test, he practices driving.
After:	What does he do **after he fails the test**?
	After he fails the test, he practices some more.
When:	What happened **when he went through the security check**?
	When he went through the security check, the alarm went off.

117

QUESTIONS & IMBEDDED QUESTIONS (Comparison of Word Order)

Question

Where	is the nearest gas station?	
How much	is the fare?	
How much	is the toll?	
How fast	is he driving?	
What bus	does she take?	
Where	did I leave	my suitcase?
When	will the train arrive?	
What	should they do?	

Imbedded Question

Do you know	where the nearest gas station is?	
Do you know	how much the fare is?	
I don't know	how much the toll is.	
We can't tell	how fast he is driving.	
I don't know	what bus she takes.	
I'm not sure	where I left	my suitcase.
Could you tell me	when the train will arrive?	
What do you think	they should do?	

CLAUSES with Optional *That*

Adjective Clauses:	When was the first time (**that**) you drove?
	Choose a car (**that**) you would like to buy.
	When was the last time (**that**) you traveled by train?
Noun Clauses:	Did you notice (**that**) your car is losing its exhaust pipe?
	You remember (**that**) you left your suitcase on the carousel.
	Do you think (**that**) the plane will arrive on time?

PREFIX: *re-* (again)

Verb

do	**re**do
take	**re**take
tell	**re**tell
test	**re**test
think	**re**think

UNIT 3

WORD FAMILIES

Verb	Noun	Adjective	Adverb
analyze	analyst	analytical	analytically
apply	application/applicant	applied	
manage	management/manager	manageable	
employ	employment/employer	employable/employed	

NOUN SUFFIXES: *-ment, -tion*

advertise**ment**
bereave**ment**
depart**ment**
dismember**ment**
employ**ment**
enforce**ment**
entertain**ment**
govern**ment**
manage**ment**
require**ment**

applica**tion**
avia**tion**
certifica**tion**
communica**tion**
compensa**tion**
competi**tion**
construc**tion**
coopera**tion**
educa**tion**

hospitaliza**tion**
occupa**tion**
posi**tion**
presenta**tion**
qualifica**tion**
recommenda**tion**
repeti**tion**
transporta**tion**

To be willing + INFINITIVE

Question

How much time **are you willing to spend** in job training?
What hours **are you willing to work**?

Are you willing to travel outside the country?

Answer

I'm willing to spend as much as I need to.

I'm willing to work any hours except third shift.
Yes, **I am**.

PASSIVE VOICE

Question

What training **is required** for the job?
What experience **is needed**?
Have you ever **been self-employed**?

Answer

On-the-job training **is provided**.
No experience **is needed**.
No, **I haven't**. I've always **been employed** by one company.

NOUN CLAUSES: *To be + that*

One good thing about my job	is	that it's close to home.
Another advantage	is	that it has good benefits.
The only disadvantage	is	that the pay is low.
The best thing about it	is	that I have a good boss.

MODALS: *Could/Should/Would*

What **could** you **list** as special skills?
What work **would** he **do** in each job?
Which job **should** he **choose?**
Should you **include** all of your work history on a job application?
What **should** you **do** if you cannot arrive on time for an interview?
What **would** he **wear** for each job?
What **would** be the advantages of each job?
What **would** the disadvantages **be?**

ADJECTIVE SUFFIX (-*al*)

manual
medical
mental
physical
technical

UNIT 4

WORD FAMILIES

Verb	Noun	Adjective	Adverb
advance	advance/advancement	advanced/advancing	
demonstrate	demonstration	demonstrable	demonstrably
	eagerness	eager	eagerly
economize	economy	economical/economic	economically
	enthusiasm	enthusiastic	enthusiastically
explode	explosion/explosive	explosive	explosively
	extravagance	extravagant	extravagantly
	prudence	prudent	prudently
resign	resignation	resigned	resignedly
	sense	sensible	sensibly
stress	stress	stressful	stressfully
waste	waste	wasteful	wastefully

NEGATIVE PREFIXES (*dis-/im-/-in/-ir/un-*)

Negative Adjective	Opposite
discourteous	courteous
impatient	patient
inflammable	flammable
irresponsible	responsible
uncertain	certain
unclear	clear
uncomfortable	comfortable
unfamiliar	familiar

ADJECTIVE SUFFIXES (*-ed /-ing*)

(*-ing*) Active

The instructions are	confusing.	
The illustration is	puzzling.	
This is	interesting	work.
I made an	embarrassing	mistake.

(*-ed*) Passive

I'm	confused	by the instructions.
I'm	puzzled	by the illustration.
I'm	interested	in this work.
I was	embarrassed	by my mistake.

ADJECTIVE SUFFIXES (*-ful/-less*)

-ful (with)   *-less* (without)

care**ful**	care**less**
thought**ful**	thought**less**
	sense**less**
waste**ful**	

ADJECTIVE SUFFIXES (-able/-ent/-eous/-ible/-ic/-ive/-ous/-tious/-y)

-able	-ent	-eous	-ible	-ic/-ical
flamm**able** comfort**able**	depend**ent**	court**eous**	combust**ible** respons**ible** sens**ible**	energet**ic** economi**cal**

-ious	-ive	-ous	-tious	-y
industr**ious**	cooperat**ive** explos**ive**	danger**ous** hazard**ous** poison**ous**	conscien**tious**	hast**y** slopp**y** worth**y**

NOUN SUFFIXES (-sion/-tion)

-sion	-tion
confu**sion** eva**sion** explo**sion**	deduc**tion** demonstra**tion** exemp**tion** explana**tion** illustra**tion** instruc**tion** promo**tion** repeti**tion** resigna**tion**

QUESTIONS & IMBEDDED QUESTIONS (Question words + Infinitive)

How do you switch	a phone call to another extension?
Where can I find	the office supplies?
When should I start	the machine?
Which should I do	first?
What should I do	about my problem at work?
Should I spend	my tax refund?

I don't know **how to switch** a phone call to another extension.
Can you tell me **where to find** the office supplies?
I'm not sure **when to start** the machine.
I don't know **which** step **to do** first.
I don't know **what to do** about my problem at work.
I haven't decided **whether to spend or to save** my tax refund.

UNIT 5

WORD FAMILIES

Verb	Noun	Adjective	Adverb
assassinate	assassination/assassin	assassinated	
brave	bravery	brave	bravely
compete	competition/competitor	competitive	competitively
	courage	courageous	courageously
defend	defense/defendant	defensive	defensively
devastate	devastation	devastating	devastatingly
elect	election/electorate	elected/elective	
entertain	entertainment/entertainer	entertaining	entertainingly
	heroism/hero	heroic	heroically
	magic/magician	magical	magically
	patriotism/patriot	patriotic	patriotically
	politics/politician	political	politically
separate	separation	separate	separately
	victory/victor	victorious	victoriously

WORD FAMILIES: Compound Nouns

- news
- newscast
- newscaster
- newsmagazine
- news media
- newsperson
- newspaper
- newsroom

ADJECTIVE CLAUSES: *Who*

That's the fireman **who rescued a whole family from a terrible fire.**
The newscaster interviewed a twelve-year-old girl **who has AIDS.**
This is the fifteen-year-old boy **who defended the elderly woman from an attacker.**
On today's news I saw the woman astronaut **who was chosen to be the captain of a space shuttle mission.**
The first witness is the woman **who saw the crime.**

REDUCING ADJECTIVE CLAUSES

Adjective Clause	Reduced
She was the news reporter **who was interviewing people at the scene**.	She was the news reporter **interviewing people at the scene**.
There are several local events **which are coming soon**.	There are several local events **coming soon**.
The fireman **who was burned in the fire** has recovered now.	The fireman **burned in the fire** has recovered now.
The young woman **who is looking at her hand** is engaged.	The young woman **looking at her hand** is engaged.
The sports event **which is on TV right now** is a championship game.	The sports event **on TV right now** is a championship game.
The toxic waste **which was dumped here last month** has been cleaned up.	The toxic waste **dumped here last month** has been cleaned up.

PASSIVE VOICE: (Present/Present Progressive/Past/Future/Present Perfect/*Can*)

Present:	What heroes **are pictured** on money?
	What martyrs **are admired** in your culture?
Present Progressive:	For what heroic acts **are** these people **being honored**?
	What natural disaster **is being shown** on each TV screen?
Past:	The boy **was shot** in the arm.
	The fireman **was** badly **burned**.
Future:	The winning team **will be honored** at a banquet.
	How many people **will be affected**?
Present Perfect:	What discoveries **have been reported** in the news recently?
	A woman **has been chosen** to be the captain of the mission.
Can (modal):	Which natural disasters **can be forecast**?
	Where **can** toxic waste **be dumped** legally?

AFRICA

ASIA AND AUSTRALIA

EUROPE

127

NORTH AMERICA, CENTRAL AMERICA, AND SOUTH AMERICA

UNITED STATES OF AMERICA (U.S.A.) AND CANADA

SPEECH EVALUATION FORM

Speaker's Name: _____
Date: _____
Speech Topic: _____

	Needs Work	Satisfactory
Organization	_____	_____
Pronunciation	_____	_____
Vocabulary	_____	_____
Eye Contact	_____	_____
Visual Aids	_____	_____

Best Part of Speech: _____
Recommendations: _____

Evaluator's Name: _____

AUDIENCE EVALUATION FORM

Speaker's Name: _____
Date: _____
Speech Topic: _____

	Needs Work	Satisfactory
Attentiveness	_____	_____
Quietness	_____	_____
Eye Contact	_____	_____
Appropriateness of Questions	_____	_____
Form of Questions	_____	_____
Number of Questions	_____	_____
Responsiveness	_____	_____

Recommendations: _____
_____

Evaluator's Name: _____

ACTIVITIES GUIDE

All of the activities in **A CONVERSATION BOOK 2**, Third Edition, as in earlier editions, are student-centered. In this edition, there are many new activities that have been structured to utilize information gaps or opinion gaps. Many activities are task-based, and all are designed to require real communication. The activities fall into three major groups: Class Activities, Group Activities, and Partner Activities. We are including here abbreviated suggestions for teaching all types of activities in the student text. For more specific suggestions for individual activities, consult the Teacher's Edition.

CLASS ACTIVITIES

Working as a whole class fosters an atmosphere of cohesion and safety. For the introduction of the lesson, it assures that all students have access to the information for the activities ahead. Other class activities take advantage of the large group for multiple opinions and experiences, especially in community activities. Any of these activities can be done in groups, if you prefer. If you are doing so, use groups of 10 to 15 students to allow for multiple input.

Class Discussion

OBJECTIVE: *To discuss individual questions as a whole class; to have students learn to understand and respect different opinions and viewpoints.*

Discuss these questions with your class. Does everyone agree?

- Ask the questions and call on different students to answer. Involve as many students as possible in the discussion. Write new vocabulary on the board as the situation allows. If there are students from different cultures, use the information to draw conclusions and teach students about different ways of life. To help structure discussions and teach note-taking skills, write a brief heading for each question on the board. Encourage students to do the same in the Activities section of their notebooks.
- Under each heading, list information you gather from the discussions.
- Review your notes and ask the students to review theirs. Together as a class at the end of the discussion, draw conclusions from the notes.

Class Game: Guess Who/What

OBJECTIVE: *To give students practice guessing through clues and prior knowledge. (This activity can be modified to be a Total Physical Response activity.)*

On a slip of paper, write. . . Make a pile. Pick a paper. Read it to the class. (Guess who wrote it!) (Ask for the answer. Whoever answers correctly picks the next paper.)

- Hand out slips of paper.
- Tell the class to write. . .
- Have students fold their slips of paper and make a pile on your desk.
- Open the first one. Read it. Guess who wrote it. (Or ask for the response.)
- Either have that student choose the next slip of paper or call on another student to choose.
- Continue as long as time and/or interest allows.

Class Survey

OBJECTIVE: *To encourage students to voice opinions and preferences, to compare their preferences with those of classmates, and to check accuracy in listening and recording answers.*

With your class, review this list of. . . Add one more. . . Interview your classmates. Report your findings to the class.

- Model the questions; have students repeat; check pronunciation. Together as a class, add one more item. Be sure students understand all the vocabulary and the objective of the activity before the activity begins.
- Have students check off their own answers in the appropriate column.
- Instruct students to circulate and ask their classmates the questions.
- Have students report their results to the class. While students are working, copy the chart on the board.
- Fill in the columns on the chart. Have students draw conclusions about the survey.
- Point out new words and have students write them in the Vocabulary section of their notebooks.

Community Activity

OBJECTIVE: *To broaden students' horizons through discovering the uses of English outside the classroom.*

Instructions will vary.

- Review the task before you ask students to work independently. These tasks can be intimidating at first; students who perform well in class may still worry about using their English outside the classroom.
- To help prepare students, role-play expected outcomes. If possible, the first time out, travel as a class to give the students confidence.
- After the assignment is completed, review in class not only the task but what happened—surprises, reactions, feelings, etc.
- Have students keep important community information in the Community sections of their notebooks.
- In an EFL class, if need be, have students do the research in their first language and then translate. Have students use the opportunity to explore where English is used in their own country and culture. This activity will give students an insight into how important the study of English is, even in the midst of their own familiar surroundings! Follow up the lesson with appropriate writing activities from **A WRITING BOOK.**

Find Someone Who

OBJECTIVE: *To encourage students to share personal information with classmates; to have students practice creating and asking yes/no questions*

Add two more items. Then interview your classmates and find someone who . . This activity is similar to the Survey activity, except that in Find Someone Who, students are searching for "Yes" answers.

- Review the vocabulary and create the Yes/No questions with the class before they start the activity. Write the questions on the board.
- Give students the grammar constructions in chunks. Review appropriate grammar from the Appendix.
- Have the class ask the questions by circulating around the class. If the class is very large, break the class into groups of 10 to 15 and have students do the activity within their group.
- When students have completed their work, have them sit in their seats.
- Review the questions and answers. Individual answers should provide interesting springboards for conversation.

School or Community Survey

OBJECTIVE: *To gather specific survey information outside class, report back, and analyze the results.*

Ask three people (in your school) these questions. Fill in the chart. Report their answers to the class. What are the total class results of the poll? (Do you see any trends?)

- Model the questions; have students repeat; check pronunciation. Together as a class, add one more item.
- Be sure students understand all the vocabulary and the objective of the activity. Discuss possible people they can survey and ways to introduce themselves and the survey.
- Rehearse together in class.
- Have students gather their information, either in the school or out in the community.
- Have students report their results, either individually to the class or to a group first, and then in groups to the whole class.
- As a class, review the results. Help students note trends. Take advantage of any conversation topics.

Speech

OBJECTIVE: *To give students practice in organizing thoughts, preparing, and giving speeches.*
Instructions will vary.

- Read the instructions aloud.
- Write the outline for a very brief speech on the board. Explain how to write an outline rather than writing out every word.
- Model the speech. Make students aware of the time limit. Have students prepare speeches at home. Help students correct their speeches. Suggest they prepare note cards so they won't be reading the speeches. Help them limit their speech to the time limit.
- Have students practice their speech with you or in small groups. Have the listeners give helpful hints on how to improve the speech. Give some hints yourself. Always phrase feedback in a positive way to encourage students and boost their confidence and self-esteem.
- Assign different students to be evaluators for different speakers.
- Evaluate the speech also. Point out general errors and problems without singling out any students.

Who Else?

OBJECTIVE: *To have students identify with some of the questions; to have students find others who identify with any of the same questions.*

With your class, add more choices. Check all the choices that apply to you. Then find classmates who have checked the same choices. Make a class chart on the board.

- Review the items with the class.
- Check for understanding of the vocabulary and the instructions. Draw a class chart (like the one in the text) on the board that is large enough to include every student's name.
- Elicit more choices. These choices will be added to the students' charts. Encourage new vocabulary.
- Allow students time to check their choices in their charts.
- Have students circulate the room, interviewing their classmates.
- When they have finished the activity, have them return to their seats.
- Have students transfer their information to the class chart on the board. Include your own responses as part of the class.
- In reviewing the activity, encourage common ground in the students. Take advantage of interesting cultural information that may emerge. Have students write new vocabulary words in the Vocabulary section of their notebooks.

GROUP ACTIVITIES

These activities promote cooperation and information exchange, as well as the opportunity to share knowledge and develop understanding in a small group setting. If possible, mix language groups and ability levels. Separate friends. Small groups encourage maximum participation before sharing discoveries with the class. Have students appoint a conversation monitor and a recorder.

Advantages/Disadvantages

OBJECTIVE: *To guide students in making judgments, voicing opinions, and analyzing in a small group.*

In groups of. . . , list the advantages and disadvantages of. . . Share your information with another group. Report the most interesting ideas to the class.
- Explain the issues.
- Divide the class into groups.
- Have each group choose a conversation monitor and a recorder. Have students discuss the issues and fill out their charts. Circulate; help as needed.
- As students are doing the task, draw the chart on the board. Ask groups to report on the results of their discussion. Fill out the chart accordingly.
- Take advantage of any interesting information that arises in the discussion to talk more about the topics.

Conversation Squares

OBJECTIVE: *To have students work cooperatively in groups of three to fill out a chart on various topics and to classify information.*

In groups of three, answer the questions. First write your own answers. Then ask your partners the questions and write their answers. Discuss your differences. Compare your group's answers with another group.
- Have students help create the questions they will ask. Write the questions on the board.
- Construct a chart on the board similar to the one in the text.
- Choose two "partners" to demonstrate. Take the "You" column for yourself.
- Put the names of your partners at the top of the chart as indicated in the text.
- Fill in your column. Ask and answer the questions as you fill out your partner's information.
- Ask others in the class the questions for more practice.
- Divide the class into groups of three and have the groups do the activity.
- When all of the groups have finished, ask different groups individual questions from the conversation squares.
- Write new vocabulary on the board for students to copy in the Vocabulary section of their notebooks.

Cross-Cultural Exchange

OBJECTIVE: *To encourage exchange of information about students' cultures; to compare cultural similarities and differences; to let students voice opinions and confusion about cultures associated with English; to encourage intercultural openness and awareness without judgment.*

In groups of. . . , choose a conversation monitor and a recorder. Discuss these questions. Compare cultures when possible. Have the recorder report the results of your discussion to the class.
- Divide the class into the suggested groups. Have each group appoint a conversation monitor and a recorder. If necessary, remind students about the function of each.
- Either have the conversation monitor ask the questions, or have students take turns asking and answering the questions. Circulate; help as needed.
- Be sure everyone's culture is represented in the discussion.
- Whenever possible, have students teach their group something interesting about their native culture, either how to say something in their native language or an interesting cultural note. This validates students' backgrounds, fosters self-esteem, and is essential in building a humanistic classroom.
- At the end of the group activity, bring the class together. Have the recorders report to the class on the results of the discussions.

Finish the Story

OBJECTIVE: *To have students work cooperatively in groups; to use creativity to complete a story and use new vocabulary.*

In groups of. . . , create an ending for this story. Then tell your ending to another group (or to the class). Answer these questions in your ending (questions will vary).

- Divide the class into the suggested groups.
- Read the instructions together.
- Go over the questions to answer, if applicable.
- Choose a conversation monitor and a recorder for each group.
- Combine groups to share endings if the class is large or if time is short. Otherwise, have each group report to the class.

Group Brainstorm

OBJECTIVE: *To encourage students to think about topics without bounds of "right" or "wrong." To tap into their prior knowledge and build skills from there.*

In groups of. . . , list all. . . Read your list to the class. Write the new words in the Vocabulary section of your notebook.

- Present the topic to be discussed.
- Explain the concept of "brainstorming"—allowing for the free flow of ideas without worrying about being restricted.
- Divide the class into groups.
- Have each group choose a recorder who will be responsible for writing down all the words or ideas.
- Instruct the groups to call out to the recorder words or ideas associated with the topic.
- Remind students to work quietly and not to comment on or judge anything being said.
- When the list is completed, have the recorders read the list to their groups.
- Advise the groups to edit their lists.
- Ask each recorder to read his/her group's list to the class. Make a class list on the board.
- Have students write any new words in the Vocabulary section of their notebooks.
- Keep the list on the board for further reference in the lesson.

Group Decision

OBJECTIVE: *To encourage sharing of preferences and opinions; to have students work cooperatively to reach consensus in situations where group members have differing preferences and opinions.*

In groups of. . . , decide. . . Report your decisions to the class. Explain why you made your decisions.

- Divide the class into groups.
- Read the instructions together.
- Be sure students understand what to do. Explain the concept of "compromise."
- Have each group agree on a decision. Circulate; help as needed.
- When the groups have completed their work, have them report their decisions to the class.

Group Discussion

OBJECTIVE: *To integrate new vocabulary into the context of students' experiences; to have students talk in small groups about an issue and to research answers; to teach them how to listen to other students, take notes, and report findings.*

In groups of. . . , answer these questions. Research any question you are not sure of. Share your information with another group. Report your answers to the class.

- Divide the class into the suggested groups. Have each group appoint a conversation monitor and a recorder. Circulate; help as needed.

- Help students use the information from their discussions to draw conclusions and learn about different ways of doing things and different ways of life.
- To help structure the conversations and teach note-taking skills, write a brief heading for each question on the board. Encourage students to do the same in the Activities section of their notebooks.
- Under each heading, list information you gather from the discussion reports.
- Review your notes and ask the students to review theirs.
- Have the recorders report the results of the discussions to the class.
- Together as a class, draw conclusions from the notes.

Group Problem Posing/Solving

OBJECTIVE: *To guide students in stating a problem; to have them work cooperatively to find a solution and to share solutions with the class.*

In groups of. . . , state each problem. What advice would you give? Report your solutions to the class.

- Divide the class into the suggested groups. Have each group choose a recorder. Instruct the groups to first decide what the problem is and how to state it clearly in one or two sentences.
- Have the recorder write down the problem. Tell the groups to decide on a solution for the problem. Circulate; help as needed.
- Have each recorder state the problem and the solution to the class.
- Have the class decide how to state the problem best and which solutions are workable.

Group Questions

OBJECTIVE: *To have students practice formulating questions; to have them ask and answer questions with another group.*

In groups of. . . , write as many questions as you can about. . . Ask another group your questions. Then answer their questions. (Read your questions to the class. Make a class list on the board. How many different questions did the class have?)

- Divide the class into small groups, each with a conversation monitor.
- Either ask the questions yourself or ask different students to ask the questions and call on various students to answer.
- Be sure all students have the opportunity to participate. Circulate; help as needed.
- As new vocabulary and important grammatical phrases arise, list them on the board.
- Have groups read their questions to the class.
- Create a class list of the questions on the board.
- Have groups ask each other some of the questions.
- When the activity has been completed, point out the new vocabulary to the students. Have them write new words and phrases in the Vocabulary section of their notebooks.

Group Role Play

OBJECTIVE: *To teach students to collaborate and create a scenario based on the conversation topic and act it out; to have them practice both verbal and non-verbal communication.*

In groups of. . ., create a role play. . .Present your role play to the class.

- Read the instructions with the class to be sure everyone understands what to do.
- Create a sample role play with the class. Act it out with volunteers.
- Ask students to write a script for some role plays; other times, have them plan the action without a script and present it extemporaneously for fluency practice.
- Divide the class into the suggested groups. Have each group plan their own role play. Circulate; help as needed.

- Have several groups present their role plays to the class.
- Note on the board any new vocabulary that arises from the role plays.
- Have students copy new words and phrases in the Vocabulary section of their notebooks.
- Discuss any interesting topics that arise during the presentations.

Group Survey

OBJECTIVE: *To have students collaborate first on the answers, then compare their answers with the whole class.*

In groups of four, answer these questions. Choose a recorder to write your answers and report to the class. What experiences do your classmates have in common? Who has a unique experience to tell about?

- Divide the class into groups of four.
- Review the questions with the class; check for understanding.
- Have groups appoint a recorder and a conversation monitor.
- Have the conversation monitor ask the questions and the recorder write the answers.
- Circulate; help where needed.
- Have each group report their answers to the class.
- Draw conclusions, make comparisons. Use the information as a springboard for discussion.

Group Vocabulary Challenge

OBJECTIVE: *To practice in combining brainstorming with discrete vocabulary recall. Cooperation and collaboration are needed to successfully complete the contest.*

In groups of. . ., list. . . Work quickly! Read your list to the class. Which group has the longest list? Make a class list on the board. Copy the new words in the Vocabulary section of your notebook.

- Divide the class into the suggested groups. If applicable, allow students to look at the illustration(s), then close their texts. (Some Challenges use the illustrations in the text, some don't.)
- Instruct students to use a page in the Vocabulary section of their notebook. Have students choose a recorder to write down the words they dictate. Give students a time allotment to complete the task. Use a stopwatch to time the contest! Circulate; help as needed.
- Remind the recorder to number the words as they are written, and to tally the total at the end of the time frame.
- Have the recorders either read the lists or write them on the board.
- Have students write the new words or phrases in the Vocabulary section of their notebooks.

Share Your Story

OBJECTIVE: *To create an awareness that everyone has a story to tell; to have the class share interesting stories and anecdotes about their own lives.*

In groups of. . . , tell about. . . Decide which story to tell the class. (Use these questions as a guide.)

- Divide the class into the suggested groups.
- Read the instructions together; check for understanding.
- If the activity includes guide questions, review the questions.
- Have students think about any experiences they have had concerning the topic.
- Encourage them to make notes before they speak so that they will remember the details.
- Circulate; help as needed.
- Have each group choose one story to tell the class.
- Have the groups help the individual student practice the story before telling the class.

Superlatives

OBJECTIVE: *To have students share and compare personal information; to have students practice creating questions and discover superlatives.*

In groups of. . . , answer these questions. Choose a recorder. Report your answers to the class.

- Divide the class into suggested groups and choose recorders.
- Read the questions together with the class.
- Ask the class what key questions they need to ask in their groups to find the superlatives.
- Write the key questions on the board. Circulate; help the groups as needed.
- Have groups report to the class.
- Decide on superlatives for the whole class.

What do you do if. . . ?

OBJECTIVE: *To have students analyze situations cooperatively and to decide on solutions to everyday dilemmas; to pool their knowledge, come to consensus, and report to the class.*

In groups of. . . , decide what to do in each situation. Share your answers with the class.

- Divide the class into the suggested groups.
- Read the problem(s) together; check for understanding. Have students appoint a recorder who will write down the solution(s) to be read to the class.
- Encourage maximum participation of all group members. Circulate; help as needed.
- Have the recorders read the groups' suggestions to the dilemmas.
- Note any new vocabulary on the board and have students write it in the Vocabulary section of their notebooks.

What do you say? What do you do?

OBJECTIVE: *To allow students the chance to try out new phrases and behavior; to have them decide what to say and what to do in everyday situations with the help of the group.*

In groups of. . . , decide what to say and do in each situation. Compare your decisions with the class.

- Divide the class into the suggested groups.
- Read the situation together; check for understanding.
- Have students work together to decide what they would do in the various situations. More than one solution is acceptable. Circulate; help as needed.
- Have several groups tell the class the results of their discussion.

What's the Story?

OBJECTIVE: *To have students work cooperatively to write a story based on the lesson's topic.*

In groups of. . . , tell a story about one of the scenes. Choose a conversation monitor and a recorder. Everyone in the group should contribute. . . .Edit the story. Tell your story to the class.

- Divide students into the suggested groups. Have students read the directions and look at the illustration, if applicable.
- Have each group select a conversation monitor and a recorder.
- Encourage students to help each other. Try to have even the reluctant or shy students participate by contributing sentences. Circulate; help as needed.
- After the stories are written, have all groups listen to their recorder read the story, make changes and corrections, and edit their story. Have each group decide whether their recorder will read the story or whether each student will read his or her sentence in turn.
- Photocopy the stories and distribute them in class the next day for students to read. Decide on categories: Which was the funniest? the saddest? the longest? the shortest? Which used the most new vocabulary words? Etc.

PARTNER ACTIVITIES

Partner activities are important because they foster face-to-face communication, one on one. Each student should get to talk 50 percent of the time and should maximize the opportunity to hold solid conversations.

Dialog Journal

OBJECTIVE: *To let students practice expressing feelings and experiences and sharing these thoughts with a partner; to have the partner respond in conversation and/or in writing.*

Write a journal entry about. . . Read your journal entry to a partner. Write a response to your partner's entry.

- Explain the task and encourage freedom of expression.
- Tell students they are going to write a dialog journal entry, then give it to a partner. The partner will respond in writing, so students have to leave space in their entry for their partner's response.
- Be sure one section of the students' notebook is labeled Dialog Journal.
- Have students do their Dialog Journal writing in class or at home.
- Have them exchange entries with a partner.
- Have the partner respond to the written selection in writing, setting up a "dialog journal." Or collect the journals and construct a dialog journal with each student. Respond with encouragement and positive feedback to their writing.

Draw with a Partner

OBJECTIVE: *To have students practice listening to a partner and follow directions; to discuss their drawings; to allow students to express their artistic creativity and to express their thoughts and feelings without words.*

Instructions will vary. Draw. . . Explain your drawing to your partner.

- Explain the tasks to the class. Check for understanding. Provide a model of what is expected. Sometimes, the worse your own art is, the better. Students will be less reluctant to share theirs if yours isn't very good.
- Divide the class into pairs, and have partners do the activity.
- Circulate; help as needed. At the same time, scout students who may be particularly skilled in drawing and will be able to share a useful drawing, either on the board, on a transparency, or on photocopies. Have several pairs report to the class on what they drew. Note new vocabulary words for students to copy into the Vocabulary section of their notebooks.

Partner Activity: *Dear Aunt Betty*

OBJECTIVE: *To have students practice analyzing personal situations and to either ask for or give advice.*

With a partner, read and discuss this letter. Together, write a response from Aunt Betty, giving advice to. . . Read your letter to the class.

- Read the problem letter together. Check for understanding.
- Divide the class into pairs.
- Have partners discuss the problem and figure out solutions. Circulate; help as needed.
- Have each pair read their solution to Aunt Betty's column.

With a partner, write to Aunt Betty, asking for advice about a. . . problem. Exchange the letter with another pair. Respond to their letter. Read their letter and your response to the class.

- Divide the class into pairs.
- Have partners decide what problem to write to Aunt Betty about and compose their letter.

- Combine pairs into groups of four.
- Have groups exchange letters and write a response. When groups have completed their task, ask several groups to read the letters to Aunt Betty and Aunt Betty's responses.

Partner Game: *"What do you remember?"*

OBJECTIVE: *To have students practice observation skills and remembering details.*

Look at (one of) the scene(s) with your partner. Remember as much as you can. Close your books. Describe the scene with your partner. List everything you can remember. Open your books and look at the scene. What did you forget?

- Discuss strategies for students to remember the details of the illustrations. Then have students close their texts.
- Divide the class into pairs.
- When all pairs have completed the activity, have them open their books and compare their lists with the illustration.
- Have several groups report their results to the class. Take notes on the board. Which pair had the longest list?

Partner Interview

OBJECTIVE: *To give students practice asking and answering, listening to and restating answers about a partner's experiences, and restating their partner's responses to other students.*

Ask a partner these questions. Then report your partner's responses to another pair of students (or to the class).

- If necessary, practice the interview questions with the students. Be sure they understand the questions and the vocabulary. Supply additional words as needed.
- Divide the class into pairs.
- Have students interview their partners. Circulate; help as needed.
- After the students conduct their interviews, have them report their partners' answers and responses to another pair.
- On the board, write new vocabulary generated from the interviews. Have students copy the new words in the Vocabulary section of their notebooks. Use the students' responses to the questions in the interviews for further discussions that may be of interest to the class.

Partner Questions

OBJECTIVE: *To give students practice formulating questions; to have them answer the questions formed; to work cooperatively with another pair with practice asking and answering.*

Write. . . questions. Ask another pair your questions. Present your questions and answers to the class.

- Explain the task.
- If necessary, do some practice question formations with the class. Divide the class into pairs.
- Allow a sufficient time frame for pairs to form their questions.
- If the activity calls for a role play, have students create a role play. Or, combine pairs into groups of four.
- Have groups ask and answer their questions. Circulate; help as needed.
- If applicable, have several pairs present their role plays to the class.

Partner Role Play

OBJECTIVE: *To have students practice and present one-on-one conversations: telephone calls, interviews, and interactions in everyday situations.*

With a partner, choose a situation. Create a role play. Present your role play to the class/to another pair.

- Divide the class into pairs.
- Generate the vocabulary needed. Leave the vocabulary on the board as a reference.
- Have students write "scripts" for their role plays. Explain that correct grammar and usage are important in formal business telephone conversations and interviews. Alternatively, have students do a more extemporaneous role play by discussing what they will say and presenting it without a script.
- Have students practice reading their "scripts" with the "read and look up" technique. (Scan the line; remember it as accurately as possible; SAY the line, don't read it. This technique helps with appropriate eye contact and body language required in English.)
- Call on several pairs to present their role plays to the class.

Partner Vocabulary Challenge

OBJECTIVE: *To have students practice combining brainstorming with discrete vocabulary recall between partners.*

With a partner, list. . . Compare your list with another pair. Combine lists. Read your combined list to the class. Which group has the longest list?

- Divide the class into pairs.
- Instruct students to use a page in the Vocabulary section of their notebooks.
- Give students a time allotment to complete the task. Circulate; help as needed.
- Remind students to number the words as they are written, and to tally the total at the end of the time frame.
- Have pairs combine their list with another pair.
- Ask groups of four to read their combined lists or write them on the board. Determine which group had the longest list. Have students add the new words and phrases to the Vocabulary section of their notebooks.

Write with a Partner

OBJECTIVE: *To have students work cooperatively to complete a written task and compare results with another pair.*

Instructions will vary.

- Explain the task to the class.
- Divide the class into pairs and have the pairs complete the task.
- Combine pairs into groups of four.
- Have groups work together to compare notes. Have groups report to the class on the results of their discussion.

ALPHABETICAL WORD LIST TO PICTURE DICTIONARY

A

abandoned, 18
accessible, 24
access road, 34
accidental death and dismemberment insurance (AD&D), 54
accident report, 28
accountant, 70
acquit, 86
acquittal, 86
acrobat, 84
add-on, 30
administrative assistant, 46
admiration, 88
admire, 88
advance, 72
advancement, 72
advocate, 18
afford, 10
affordable, 10
agriculture, 42
aid, 92
air conditioner, 8
air travel, 38
aisle seat, 38
alert, 62
alternate-side parking, 20
amateur athlete, 82
amazed, 16
analytical, 48
analyze, 48
anchorperson, 78
annual, 54
annual income, 70
anxiety, 58
anxious, 58
applicant, 52
apply, 52
apt. (apartment), 6
armed, 92
arrive, 36
article, 78
arts, 42
as good as new, 10
as is, 6
assassinate, 94
assassination, 94
assault, 86
assess, 12
assume, 60
athlete, 82
athletic, 82
at the scene, 78
attorney, 86

auditor, 70
auto worker, 46
avail. (available), 6
availability, 52
avalanche, 80
awkward, 58

B

back in, 26
back seat, 34
back taxes, 70
back up, 26
bad attitude, 62
bad credit, 68
bad deal, 30
baggage carousel, 38
baggage cart, 38
baggage claim, 38
bag groceries, 62
bailiff, 86
balance beam, 82
ballot, 94
ballot box, 94
banking, 42
barrier, 34
bath. (bathroom), 6
battle, 92
bdrm. (bedroom), 6
beach house, 32
beaker, 64
beauty care, 42
belongings/possessions, 14
benefits package, 54
best offer, 31
billboard, 34
bimonthly, 54
biweekly, 54
blizzard, 80
blood alcohol level, 28
blow a fuse, 8
blow-dryer, 8
blow up, 64
blue collar, 46
board, 36
boarded-up, 18
boarding pass, 38
bodyguard, 94
bonus, 54
brand new, 10
brave, 88
bravery, 88
breakable, 14
breakthrough, 92
Breathalyzer test, 28
bronze medal, 82

bsmt. (basement), 6
bucket seats, 30
budget, 68
build, 48
builder, 48
bulletin, 78
bulletin board, 50
bump, 14
bumper-to-bumper, 24
bungalow, 32
burn down, 80
burst, 64
bus shelter, 24
bus station, 36

C

cable network news, 78
campaign, 94
candidate, 94
capital punishment, 86
car crash, 90
car dealer, 30
career change, 72
career decision, 72
career objective, 52
career opportunity, 72
career path, 72
career training, 72
careful, 62
careless, 62
car pool, 24
carpool, 24
car pool lane, 24
carry-on bag, 38
castle, 32
catastrophe, 80
catch up, 76
cause, 88
cautious, 16
celebrity, 84
cell, 86
cellar, 4
certification, 46
chain lock, 16
challenge, 48
challenging, 48
champion, 76
championship, 76
change a tire, 28
charitable, 16
charity, 16
check, 60
check baggage, 38
check-in counter, 38
chemical experiment, 64
child care, 54

city withholding tax, 66
claim check, 38
clarification, 60
clarify, 60
classical music, 84
classified advertisement (ad), 50
class news, 76
cleanup, 90
clean-up campaign, 20
clerical, 46
clock in, 62
clown, 84
coach, 36
collapse, 80
colleague, 58
collection, 16
collide, 28
collision, 28
combustible, 64
combustion, 64
commentator, 82
commerce, 42
commission, 54
commit, 86
common sense, 68
communications, 42
commuter, 24
compact car, 30
compensation, 54
compete, 82
competition, 82
competitive, 82
complicated, 58
computation, 70
compute, 70
cond. (condition), 6
condo (condominium), 6
conduct, 84
conductor (symphony), 84
conductor (train), 36
confused, 60
confusion, 60
congestion, 2
conscientious, 62
construction site, 48
contact, 52
contract, 54
convenience, 4
conveyor belt, 64
convict, 86
conviction, 86
coordinate, 48
countryside, 2
courage, 88
courageous, 88

142

courteous, 62
courtroom, 86
cozy, 4
cpt. (carpet), 6
cramped, 4
crate, 14
credit rating, 68
credit risk, 68
credit union, 66
crime in the news, 86
crime watch, 20
criminal, 86
crush, 62
curb, 26
current, 8
current event, 78
customized, 4
customs, 38
customs declaration form, 38
cut off, 8

D

daily commute, 24
damage, 12
deadline, 70
deadly, 80
deadly weapon, 86
debate, 94
debt, 68
decent condition, 10
decorate, 4
dedicated, 88
deductible, 70
deduction, 66
defend, 86
defendant, 86
defense, 86
delicate, 14
deliver newspapers, 16
democracy, 94
democratic, 94
demonstrate, 60
demonstration, 60
dent, 28
dental coverage, 54
depart, 36
dependent, 70
dependent coverage, 54
design, 42
destination, 36
destroy, 80
destruction, 80
detour, 24
devastating, 80
dial tone, 8
dictator, 94
dictatorship, 94
die for, 88
dilapidated, 18
diligent, 62
dining car, 36

direct deposit, 66
director, 52
discontinue, 8
discourteous, 62
disembarkation card, 38
dishw. (dishwasher), 6
disposable income, 68
disrepair, 18
distressed, 36
distrust, 16
distrustful, 16
dn. pmnt. (down payment), 6
dog bite, 12
doing a good job, 62
door knocker, 16
door-to-door, 16
double-check, 60
driver education, 26
driver license, 26
driving instructor, 26
driving manual, 26
driving under the influence, 28
drought, 80
drunk driving, 28
dry up, 80
dumpsite, 90
dwelling, 12

E

eager, 58
early retirement, 54
earn, 66
earthquake, 80
economical, 30
economize, 68
economy car, 30
ecstatic, 76
elated, 76
elec. (electricity), 6
elect, 94
election, 94
elementary school teacher, 48
embarkation card, 38
embarrassed, 58
embrace, 76
emission, 28
employee contribution, 66
employment agency, 50
employment counselor, 50
entertain, 84
entertainer, 84
entertaining, 84
entertainment, 42
entertainment expenses, 68
entertainment news, 84
enthusiasm, 58
enthusiastic, 58

entry level, 50
erupt, 80
eruption, 80
escape, 80
evacuate, 80
evacuation, 80
exact change lane, 34
excel. (excellent), 6
executive, 46
exempt, 70
exemption, 70
exhaust, 28
exotic, 32
expect, 60
expectation, 60
expenditure, 68
expenses, 68
experienced, 26
experience necessary, 50
explode, 64
explosion, 64
explosive(s), 65
expressway/freeway, 34
extension cord, 8
extravagance, 68
extravagant, 68
extra-wide, 4

F

fail, 26
fair, 10
fall apart, 90
family entertainment, 84
family reunion, 34
famine, 92
faraway places, 32
farewell, 14
farmhouse, 2
fearful, 16
Federal Insurance Contributions Act (FICA), 66
federal withholding tax, 66
fender bender, 28
fighting, 92
figure out, 60
figure skating, 82
file a tax return, 70
fill up, 34
finalist, 82
financial responsibility, 68
fire damage, 12
fire hazard, 18
first impression, 52
first shift, 46
flammable, 64
flask, 64
flat tire, 28
flight attendant, 38
floor covering, 4
fncd. (fenced), 6

follow, 60
food service, 42
forecast, 80
forest fire, 80
Form 1040, 70
Form 1040EZ, 70
Form W-2, 70
four-by-four (4x4), 30
four-door, 30
friendliness, 20
front page, 78
full-service station, 34
fumes, 64
functional, 10
furnace, 8
furnish, 4
furnishings, 4
fuse box, 8

G

gang, 18
gate, 38
ghetto, 18
Girl Scout, 16
give notice, 72
glassware, 14
gold medal, 82
good attitude, 62
good credit, 68
good deal, 30
good sense, 68
government, 42
graffiti, 18
grass-roots organization, 20
gridlock, 24
gross earnings, 66
gross pay, 66
group insurance, 54
guilty, 86

H

hammock, 32
handgun, 86
handle, 4
hang out, 18
hang wallpaper, 4
hardworking, 62
haste, 58
hasty, 58
haul, 14
headline, 78
head-on collision, 90
health care industry, 42
health hazard, 90
heavy equipment operator, 48
heavy traffic, 24
help out, 20
help wanted sign, 50
hero, 88
heroic, 88

143

heroism, 88
high-rise, 2
highway, 34
highway patrol, 34
hijack, 92
hike, 32
hiker, 32
hire, 52
homecoming, 76
homeless, 18
homeowner, 12
honor, 88
hospital worker, 46
hostage, 92
hot water heater, 8
household goods, 14
housing development, 2
ht. (heat), 6
hug, 76
human interest story, 90
humanitarian, 92
human resources, 52
hurricane, 80

I
ignite, 64
illegal dumping, 90
illustrate, 60
illustration, 60
immigration, 38
impatience, 58
impress, 68
incl. (included), 6
income, 54
income tax, 70
independent, 48
indoor sport, 82
industrious, 62
industry, 42
inexperienced, 26
inflammable, 64
in-flight meal, 38
inform, 36
information board, 36
information booth, 36
initiative, 62
inner city, 18
innocent, 86
inquire, 50
inspector, 46
instruction manual, 60
instructions at work, 60
insurance adjustor, 12
insurance coverage, 12
insurance deduction, 66
insurance policy, 54
insurance premium, 54
interested, 62
interesting, 48
Internal Revenue Service (IRS), 70
international competition, 82
international incident, 92
interstate, 34
interview, 52
interviewer, 52
intimidate, 58
intimidating, 58
intoxicated, 28
intoxication, 28
ironing board, 8
issue, 26

J
jack, 28
jack up, 28
jail, 86
job application, 52
job lead, 50
job listing, 50
job offer, 52
job opening, 50
job qualification, 50
job reference, 52
job search, 50
jobs in your community, 42
job training, 48
junk, 18
juror, 86
jury, 86
justice, 86

K
kidnap, 90
kitch. (kitchen), 6
kneeling bus, 24
knock over, 26
knowledgeable, 58

L
laboratory, 64
labor union, 66
land, 2
landlady, 10
landlord's responsibility, 10
late penalty, 70
laundr. (laundry room), 6
lava, 80
law enforcement, 42
lawn mower, 16
lawyer, 86
leader, 88
leaky, 10
leash law, 20
leave behind, 14
leave of absence, 54
leaving a job, 72
leer, 72
legislature, 94
level, 80
liability, 12
liable, 12
life insurance, 54
limited engagement, 84
litter, 18
live above one's means, 68
live broadcast, 78
live within one's means, 68
loc. (location), 6
local, 90
local issue, 90
local news, 90
locomotive, 36
log cabin, 2
loiter, 18
looking for a job, 50
loss of property, 12
lot, 2
low pay, 72
lugnut, 28
lug wrench, 28
lunch break, 58

M
magic, 84
magical, 84
magician, 84
main road, 34
maintain, 10
maintenance, 10
major appliance, 10
make, 30
make a deal, 30
make an inquiry, 50
makeshift, 10
management, 46
mandatory insurance, 12
manual labor, 48
manufacturing, 42
march, 94
martyr, 88
maternity leave, 72
medal, 88
medalist, 82
media, 78
medical coverage, 54
medical technician, 48
Medicare tax, 66
melt, 10
memorial, 88
men's apparel/fashion, 48
metal detector, 38
meter, 8
military, 92
military coup, 94
mini-blinds, 4
minimum wage, 52
minor accident, 28
misplace, 14
missing, 90
mistake, 58
mistrust, 16
mistrustful, 16
misunderstand, 60
mixed pairs, 82
mix up, 60
mix-up, 60
mo. (month), 6
model, 30
moderation, 68
modified fixtures, 4
money management, 42
monthly, 54
monument, 88
motor home, 2
motorist, 24
motor vehicle bureau (MVB), 26
mountain bike, 32
mountain climbing, 32
move away, 72
mug, 86
mugging, 86
multiple-family dwelling, 2
multi-vehicle accident, 90
murder, 86
MVP (Most Valuable Player), 76

N
natural disaster, 80
neglect, 18
negotiable, 30
negotiate, 30
neighborly, 20
net earnings, 66
newscast, 78
newscaster, 78
newsmagazine, 78
news media, 42
newsperson, 78
nick, 14
night clerk, 34
night shift, 46
no experience required, 50
no-fault/liability insurance, 28
no money down, 31
non-negotiable, 66
nonpayment, 8
nonresident, 70
notification, 8
notify, 8
nr. (near), 6

O
obligation, 10
occupant, 4
occupation, 42
occupied, 20
office work, 42
office worker, 46

144

official, 94
off-street parking, 20
oil heat, 8
oil spill, 92
oil tank, 8
Olympics, 82
one-story, 2
on-line news, 78
on location, 78
open house, 6
optimism, 20
option, 30
optional, 30
optional insurance, 12
organize, 14
outdoor sport, 82
outlook, 20
overcrowded, 90
overgrown, 16
overhead compartment, 38
overjoyed, 76
overload a circuit, 8
overlook, 60
overpay, 70
overspend, 68
overthrow, 94
overtime, 46
overwhelmed, 76
overworked, 72
owe, 68
own, 2
ownr. (owner), 6

P

pack, 14
package tour, 32
packing box, 14
paid vacation, 54
paper jam, 58
parallel park, 26
paraprofessional, 48
pass, 26
passing lane, 24
patriot, 88
patriotic, 88
patriotism, 88
payday, 66
pay for, 16
pay interest, 70
pay period, 66
paystub, 66
pay taxes, 70
performer, 84
perplexed, 60
personal news, 76
personal safety, 18
personnel department, 52
petition, 18
photography, 42
picket, 94
pileup, 90

pitch in, 20
plug, 8
plug in, 8
plumbing, 10
pole vault, 82
political party, 94
politician, 94
politics, 94
pollutant, 90
pollute, 90
polluter, 90
porter, 36
position, 50
position desired, 52
post, 50
powerful, 80
premium, 12
presentation, 48
pride, 62
privacy, 4
private sector, 42
probationary period, 58
professional, 48
professional athlete, 82
profit sharing, 54
proper appearance, 52
property, 2
prosecute, 86
prosecution, 86
protect, 88
protection, 12
protective gear, 64
protest, 94
protestor, 94
prudent, 68
public service, 42
pump gas, 34
punctual, 52
punish, 86
punishment, 86
put away, 14
puzzled, 60

R

rainbow, 20
rally, 94
ranch house, 2
reach, 62
real estate, 2
real estate agent, 6
realtor, 6
recoil, 64
recommend, 50
recommendation, 50
recreational vehicle, 2
recruit, 52
recruiter, 52
recruitment, 52
Red Cross, 92
redecorate, 4
refrig. (refrigerator), 6
refugee, 92

refurbish, 20
registration desk/ front desk, 34
regret, 72
rehabilitate, 20
rehabilitation, 20
reimburse, 54
reimbursement, 54
remodel, 4
remuneration, 54
renew, 26
renewal, 26
renovate, 20
renovation, 20
rental, 2
rental car, 32
repair cost, 12
repeat, 60
replacement cost, 12
reporter, 78
report the news, 78
repossess, 68
representative, 94
request, 60
requirement, 52
rescuer, 80
research scientist, 92
residence, 2
resident, 70
resign, 72
resignation, 72
restricted lane, 24
rest stop, 34
resume, 52
retail sales, 42
retake, 26
retirement contribution, 66
reunion, 76
reunite, 76
reverse, 26
rewire, 8
riot, 94
risk, 88
rms. (rooms), 6
road crew, 24
roadkill, 34
road repair, 24
roadside motel, 34
road test, 26
road trip, 34
rob, 86
robbery, 86
roof rack, 30
roomy, 4
route map, 24
rubble, 80
run down, 18
run out, 8
run over, 18
rushed, 58
rush hour, 24

S

sacrifice, 88
saint, 88
salary, 54
salary after taxes, 66
sales pitch, 30
satellite news, 78
savings plan, 54
scenery, 32
scenic, 32
scientific discovery, 92
sea, 32
seasonal layoff, 72
second shift, 46
secretarial, 46
security, 42
security check, 38
sedan, 30
seek employment, 50
self-employed, 46
self-improvement, 72
semidetached, 2
semi-finalist, 82
sensible, 68
sentence (punishment), 86
separation, 76
sequence, 60
serviceable, 10
service industry, 42
sexual advance, 72
shake, 80
shatter, 64
shift, 46
shipping, 42
shock, 76
shoot/fire, 64
shoulder, 34
show how, 58
showroom, 30
signal, 24
silver medal, 82
simple pleasures, 68
single-family dwelling, 2
skating rink, 82
skilled, 48
skip a step, 60
sleeper car, 36
slip and fall, 76
small town, 2
smoke damage, 12
snowcapped, 32
sober, 20
Social Security (FICA), 66
solve problems, 48
space, 2
spacious, 4
spare tire, 28
speaker, 94
special delivery, 16
special meal, 38
special needs, 4

145

special occasion, 76
specific, 60
specifically, 60
speeding ticket, 34
spend, 68
spending money, 68
spendthrift, 68
splurge, 68
sports event, 82
sports news, 82
sports utility vehicle, 30
sprawling, 2
stack, 62
stadium, 82
stage, 84
standard deduction, 70
star, 84
stare, 72
starting a new job, 58
starting salary, 52
starvation, 92
starve, 92
statement of earnings and deductions, 66
state withholding tax, 66
station, 78
station attendant, 34
station wagon, 30
statue, 88
steer, 26
sticker price, 30
stolen property, 12
storage space, 4
store, 4
storeroom, 4
storm damage, 12
stranger, 16
stray dog, 18
street light, 18
strength, 88
stressful, 72
stuck in traffic, 24
studio, 6
suburb, 2
sun roof, 30
superintendent (super), 10
supplies, 92
supporter, 94
survival, 80
symphony orchestra, 84

T

tail pipe, 28
take for granted, 60
take-home pay, 66
tank, 92
task, 58
taxable income, 70
tax credit, 70
tax evasion, 70
tax form(s), 70
taxpayer, 70

tax withheld, 70
teammate, 76
teamwork, 62
tears of joy, 76
technical, 48
technical training, 72
telecast, 78
telephone interview, 50
tenant's rights, 10
tenement, 2
terminal, 36
terrify, 80
terrorism, 92
terrorist, 92
testify, 86
testimony, 86
theme park, 84
the right job for you, 48
thermostat, 8
third shift, 46
Third World, 92
thrill, 76
thrilled, 76
thrilling, 76
throw one's back out, 64
thunderous, 80
ticket, 28
ticket agent, 36
ticket counter, 36
ticket stub, 38
tidal wave, 80
tightrope walker, 84
tilt, 38
time change, 36
time-consuming, 24
timesaving, 24
time zone, 36
toll, 34
toll booth, 34
toll road, 34
top story, 78
tornado, 80
tourism, 42
towering, 80
town house, 2
toxic waste, 90
track and field, 82
traffic cone/pylon, 26
traffic jam/tie-up, 24
train platform, 36
train station, 36
transp. (transportation), 6
transport, 14
trapeze artist, 84
travel agent, 32
traveler, 32
tray, 38
tray table, 38
trial, 86
triumph, 76
trophy, 76
truth in advertising, 30

turnpike, 34
two-door, 30
two-family dwelling, 2
two-story, 2

U

uncertain, 58
unclear, 58
under construction, 24
underdeveloped, 92
underemployed, 46
underpaid, 72
unexpected, 16
unfamiliar, 58
unforgettable moment, 76
union dues, 66
unload, 14
unpaid leave, 54
unqualified, 46
unsafe, 18
unsafe conditions, 90
unskilled, 48
unwrap, 14
upright position, 38
urban renewal, 20
used, 10
used car, 31
used car lot, 30
utility trailer, 14
utils. (utilities), 6

V

vacationer, 32
vagrant, 18
van, 30
vandal, 18
vandalism, 18
vendor, 42
verdict, 86
veteran, 88
victorious, 76
victory, 76
view, 32
village, 2
violate, 28
violation, 28
vision test, 26
vista, 32
volcano, 80
vote, 94

W

w. (with), 6
wage(s), 54
waiting area, 36
walk-up, 2
war, 92
warning sign, 64
wary, 16
waste, 68
wasteful, 68

water damage, 12
weeds, 18
weekly, 78
well qualified, 52
wheelchair, 4
wheelchair access, 24
white collar, 46
window seat, 38
window treatment, 4
wipe out, 92
wiring, 8
witness stand, 86
word of mouth, 50
work environment, 48
work habits, 62
work history, 52
working conditions, 72
working order, 10
world news, 92
wrap, 14
written test, 26
w/w (wall-to-wall), 6

Y

yd. (yard), 6
your occupation, 46
youth hostel, 32